I0462154

Real World

Colouring Book

For Advanced Users & Adults

50 Images

Created From Real Life Photos
For You To Colour As You Please.

ISBN 978-0-359-80156-5
90000
9 780359 801565

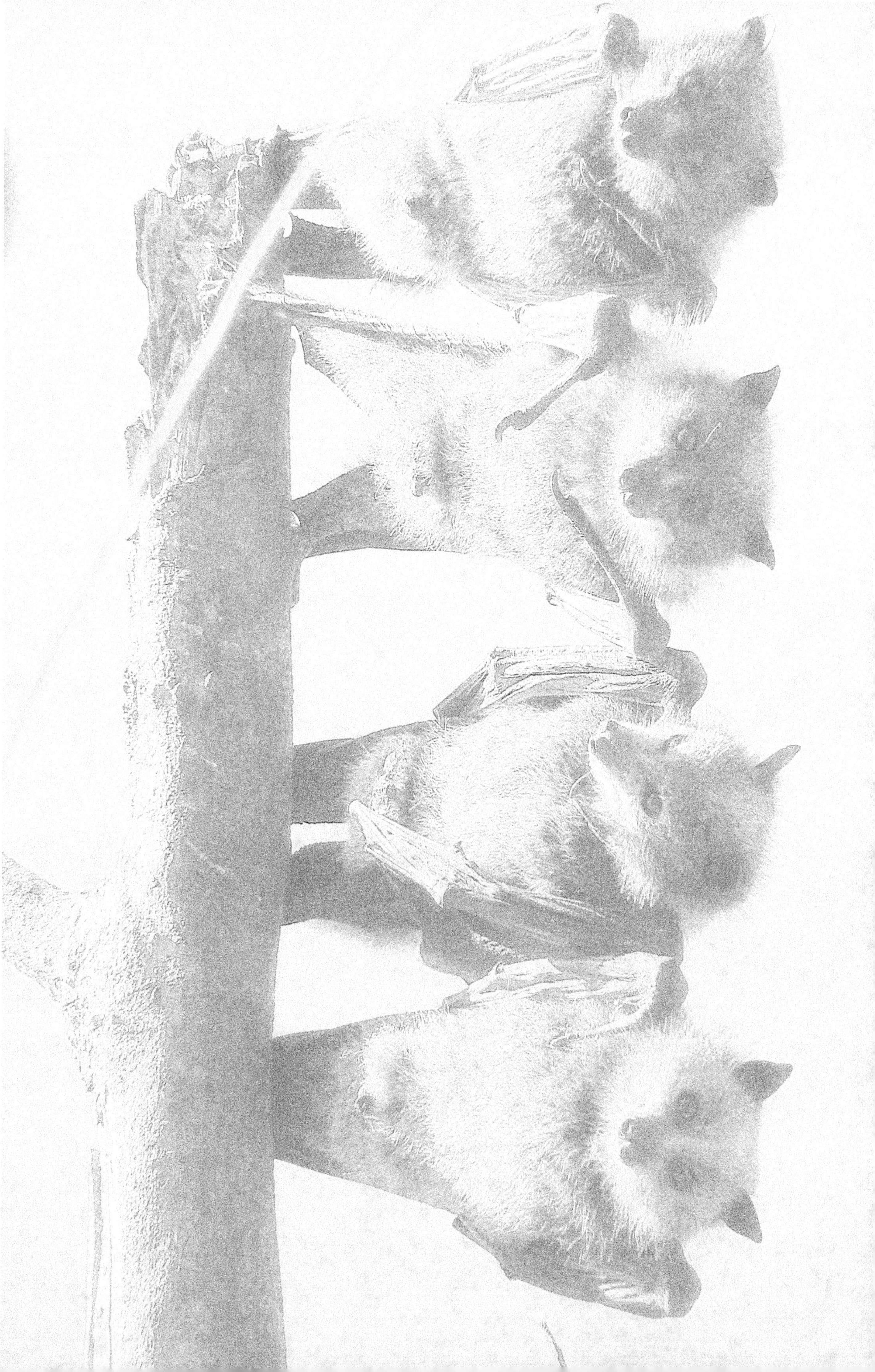

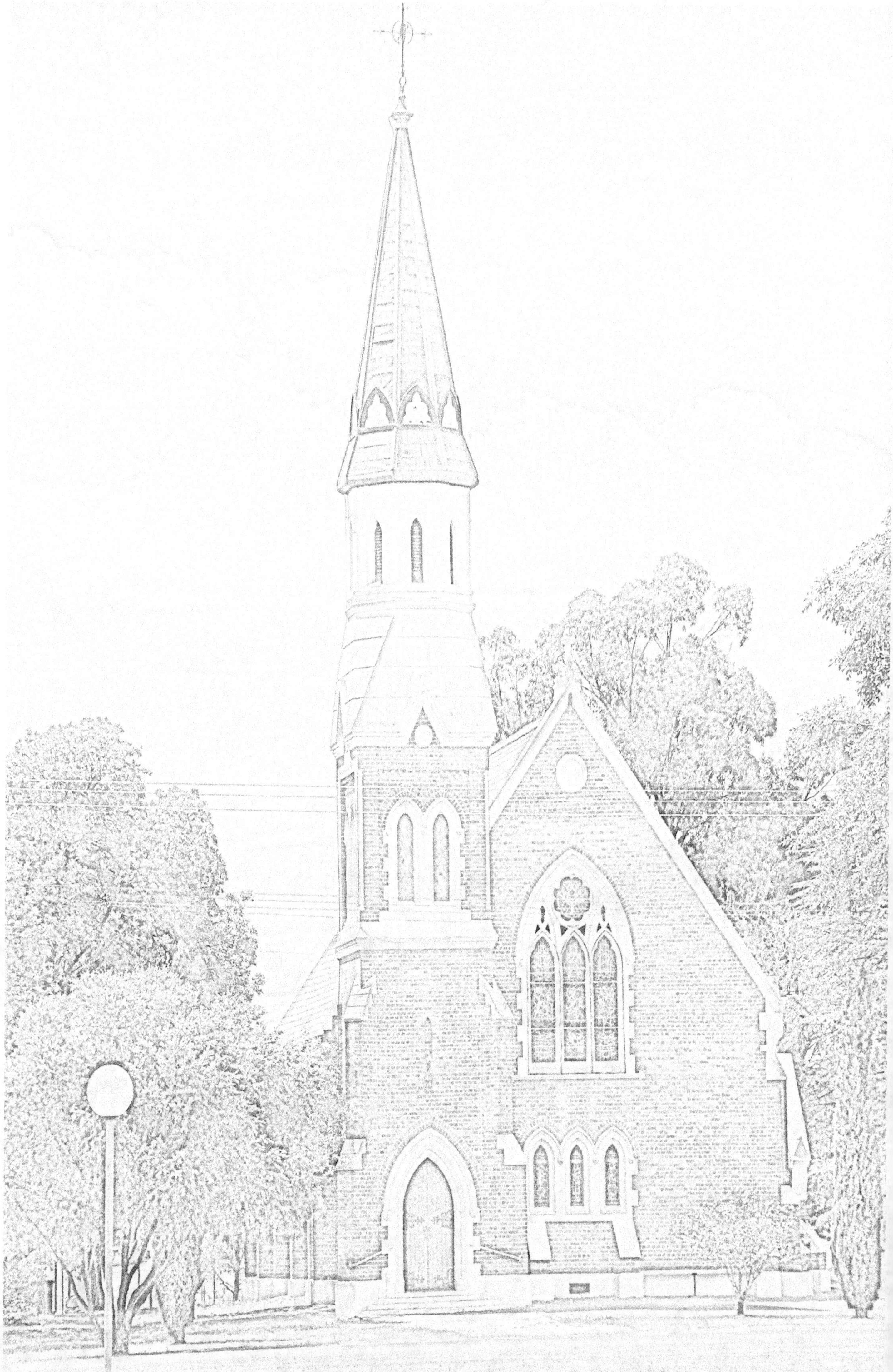

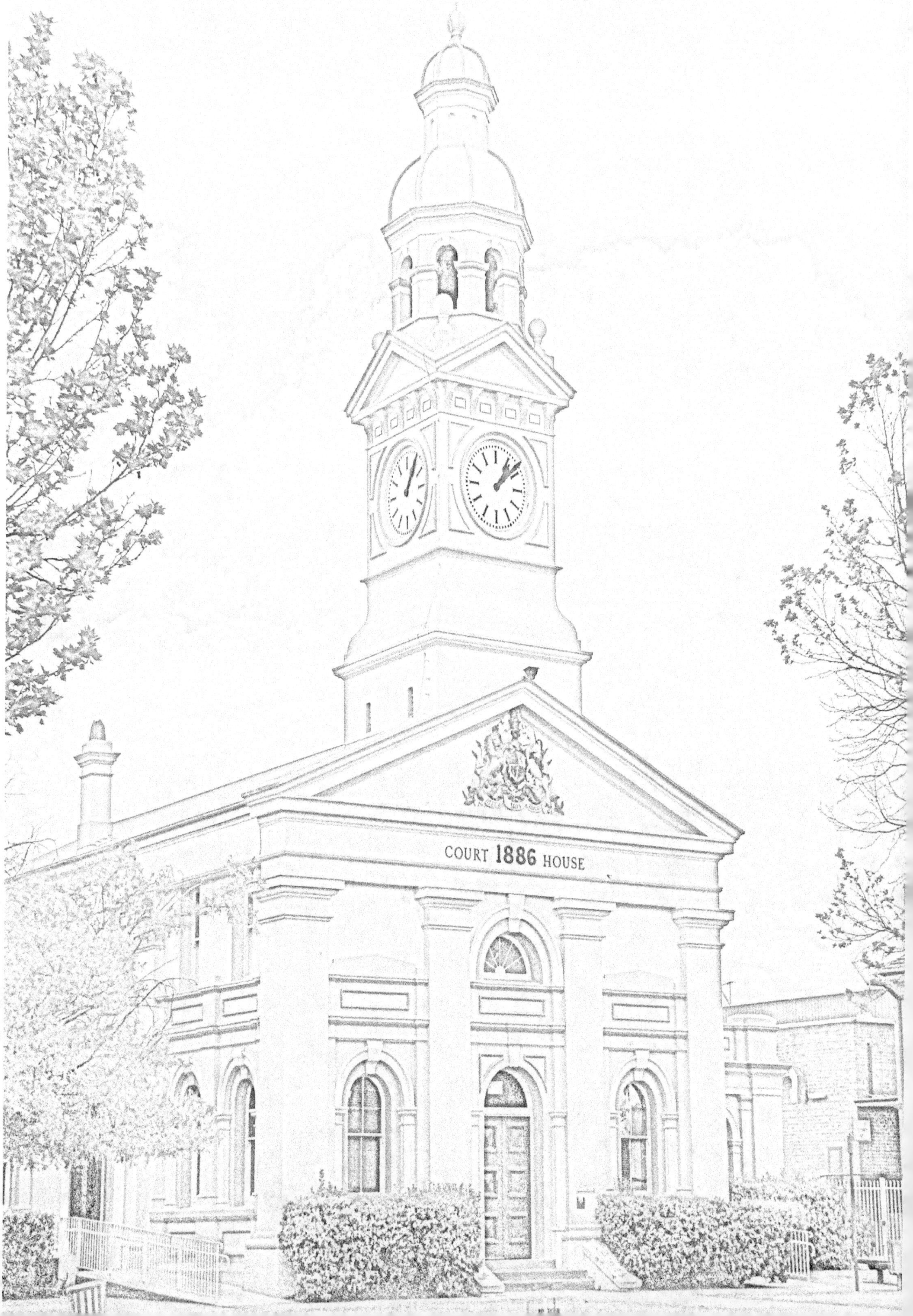
COURT 1886 HOUSE

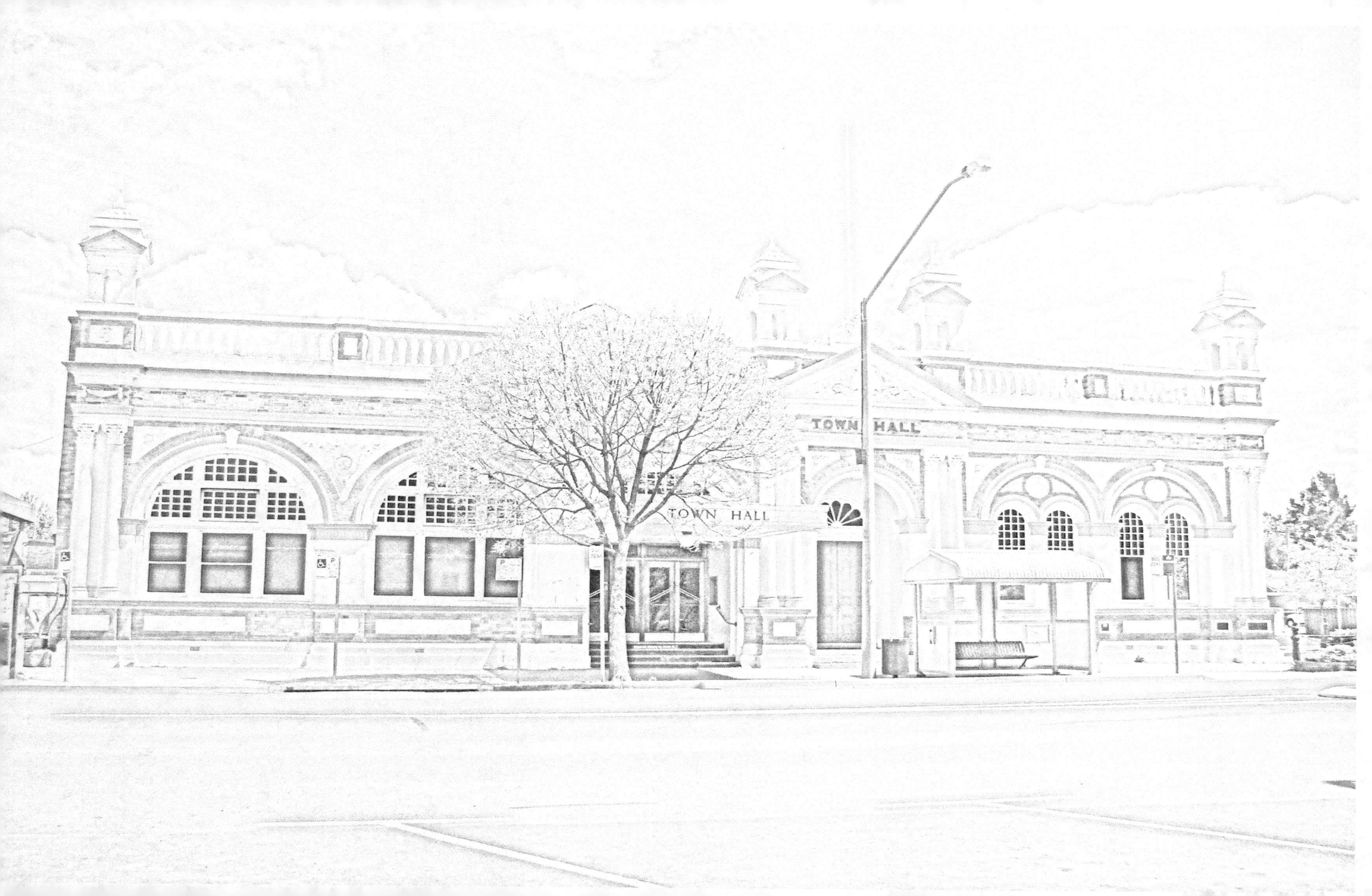
TOWN HALL
TOWN HALL

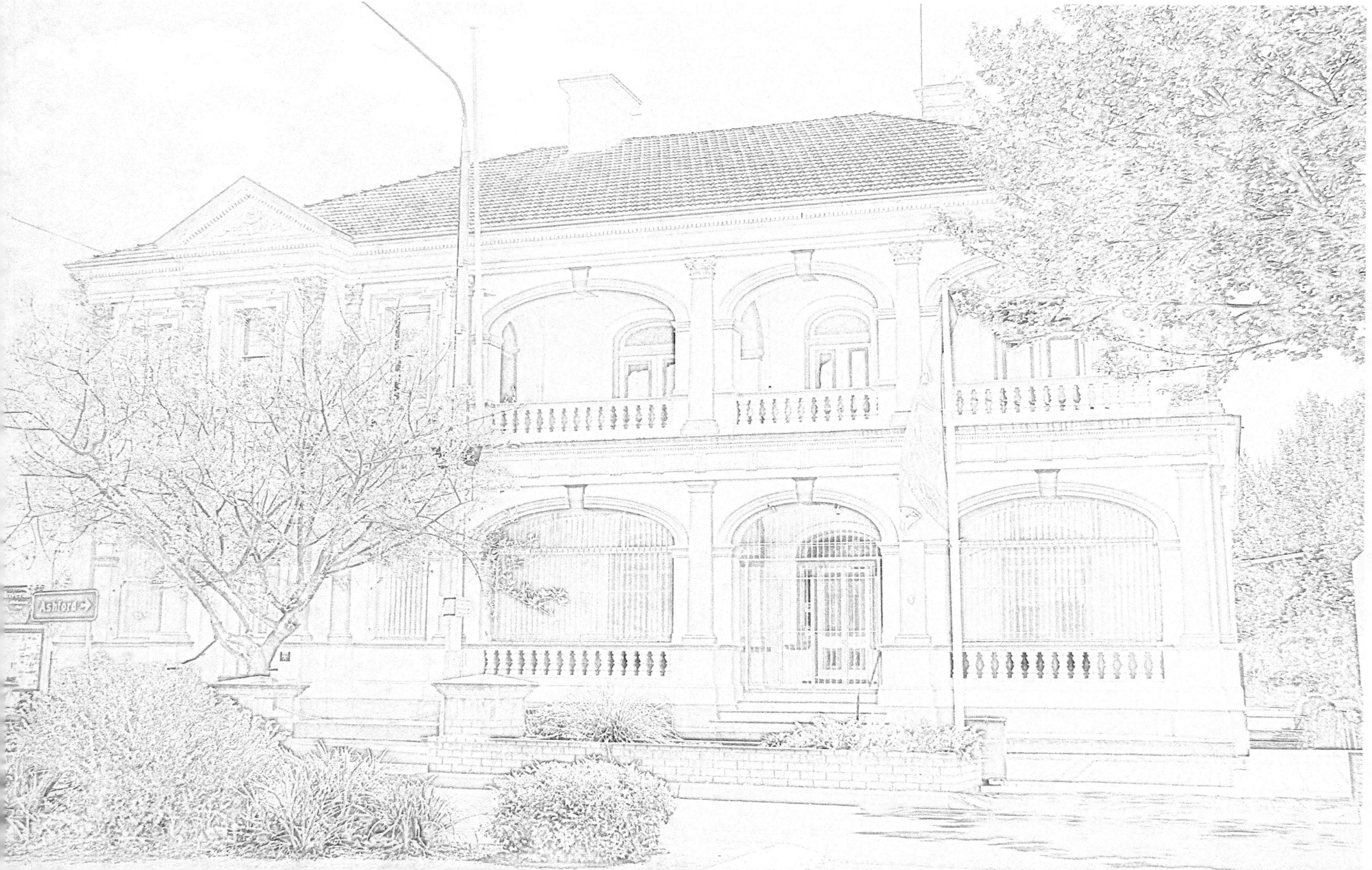
Ashford

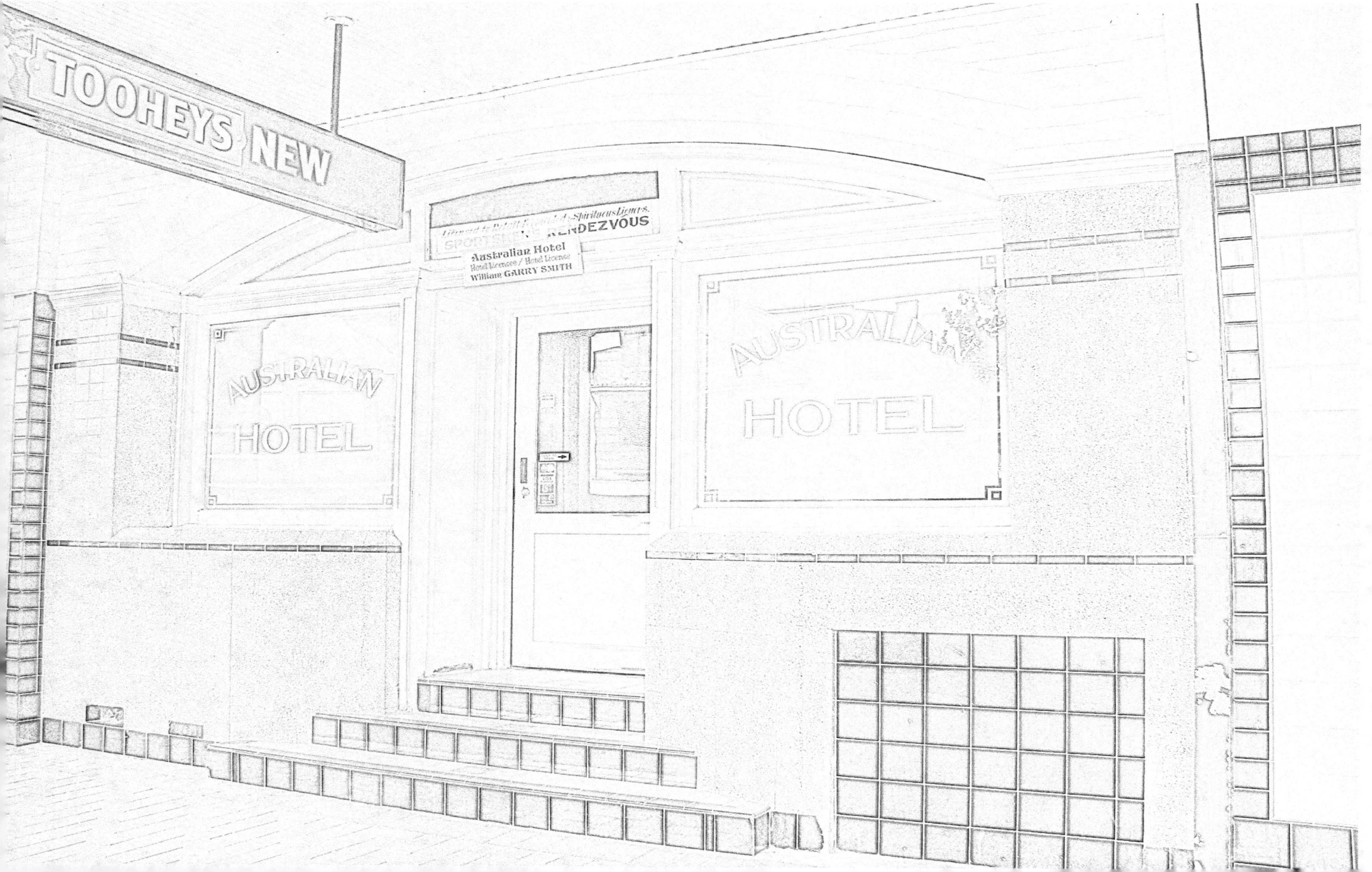
TOOHEYS NEW
SPORTSMEN'S RENDEZVOUS
Australian Hotel
Hotel Licensee / Hotel License
William GARRY SMITH
AUSTRALIAN
HOTEL
AUSTRALIAN
HOTEL

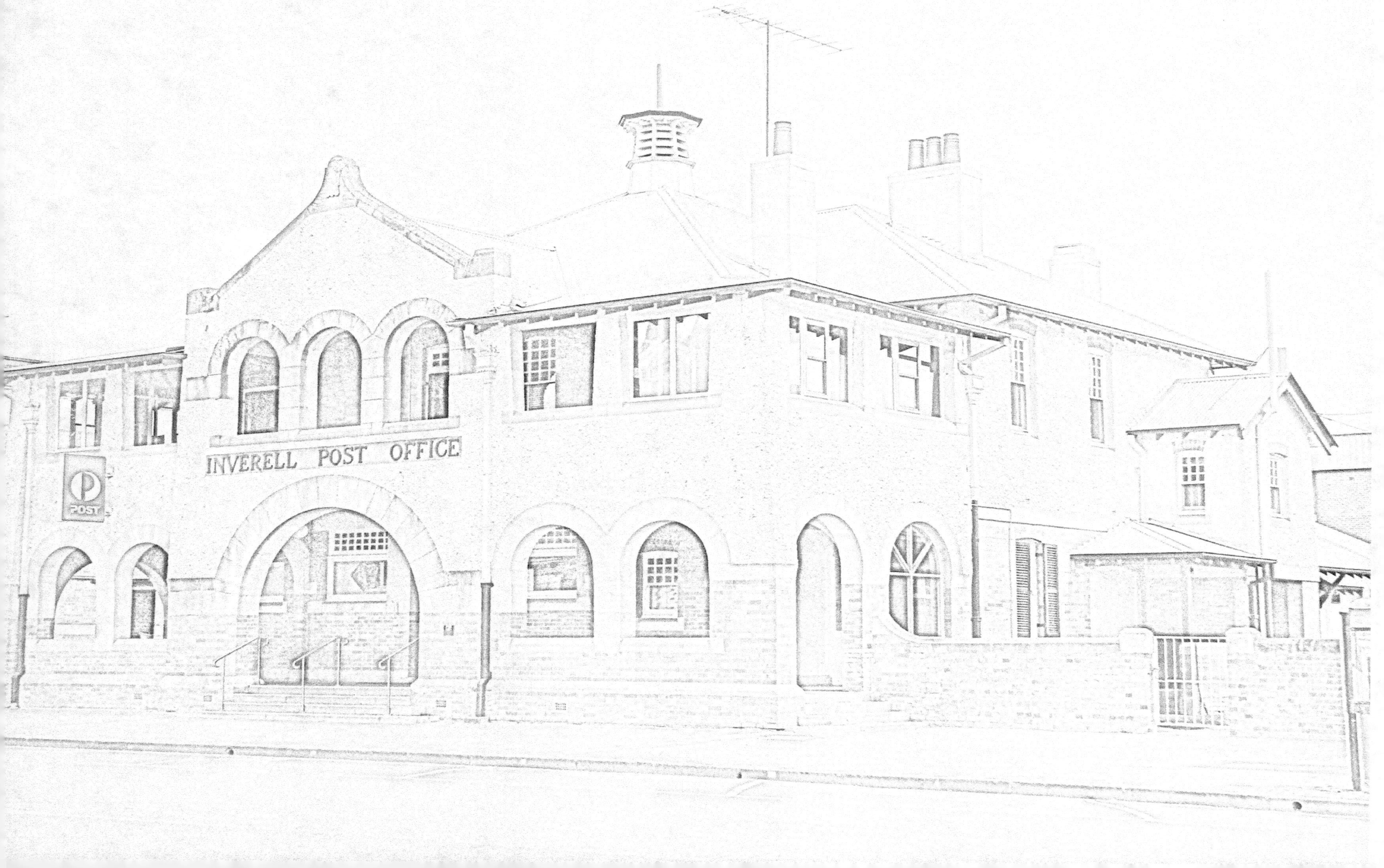
INVERELL POST OFFICE
POST

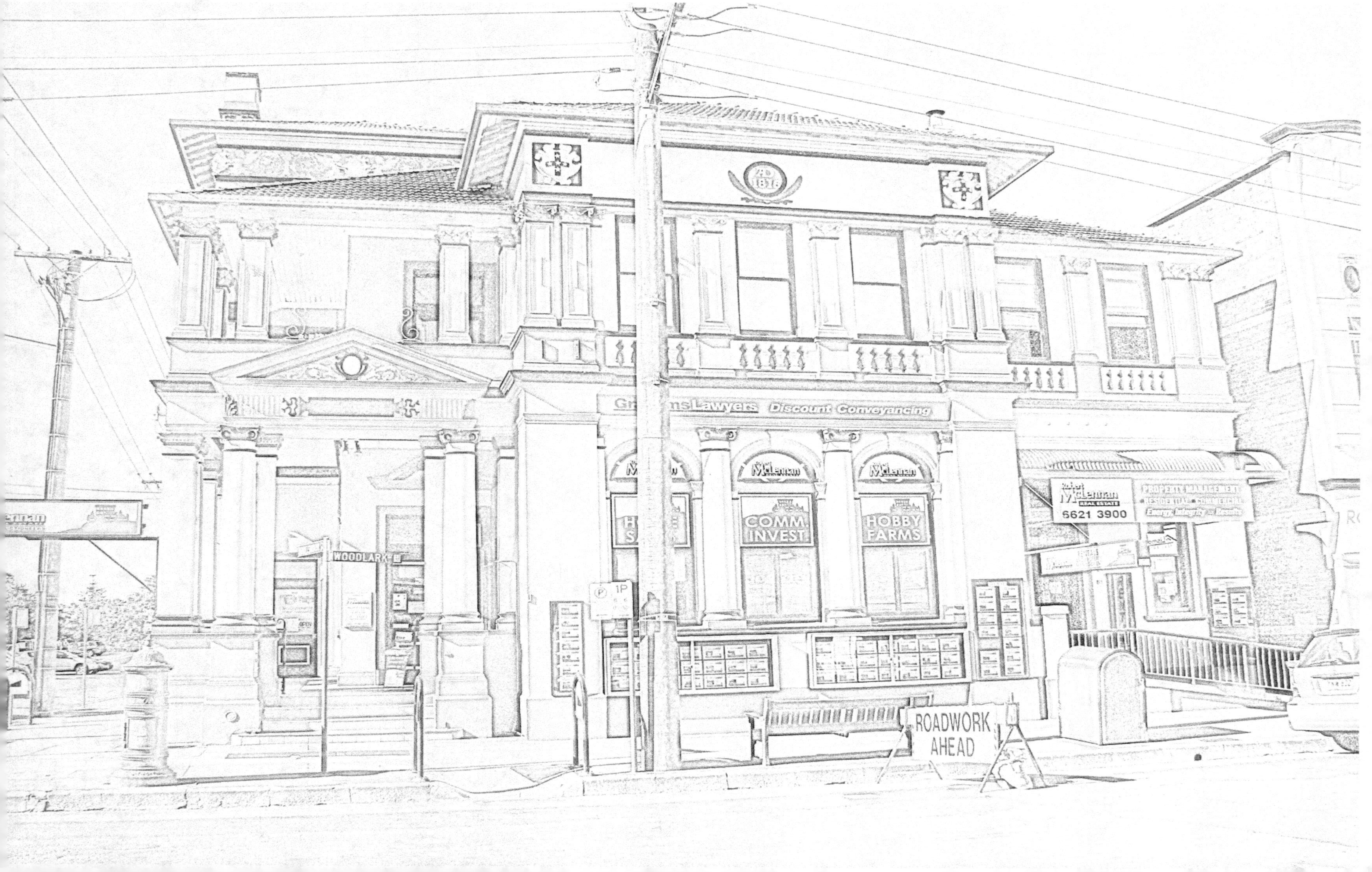

Discount Conveyancing
COMM INVEST
HOBBY FARMS
6621 3900
PROPERTY MANAGEMENT
WOODLARK
1P
ROADWORK
AHEAD

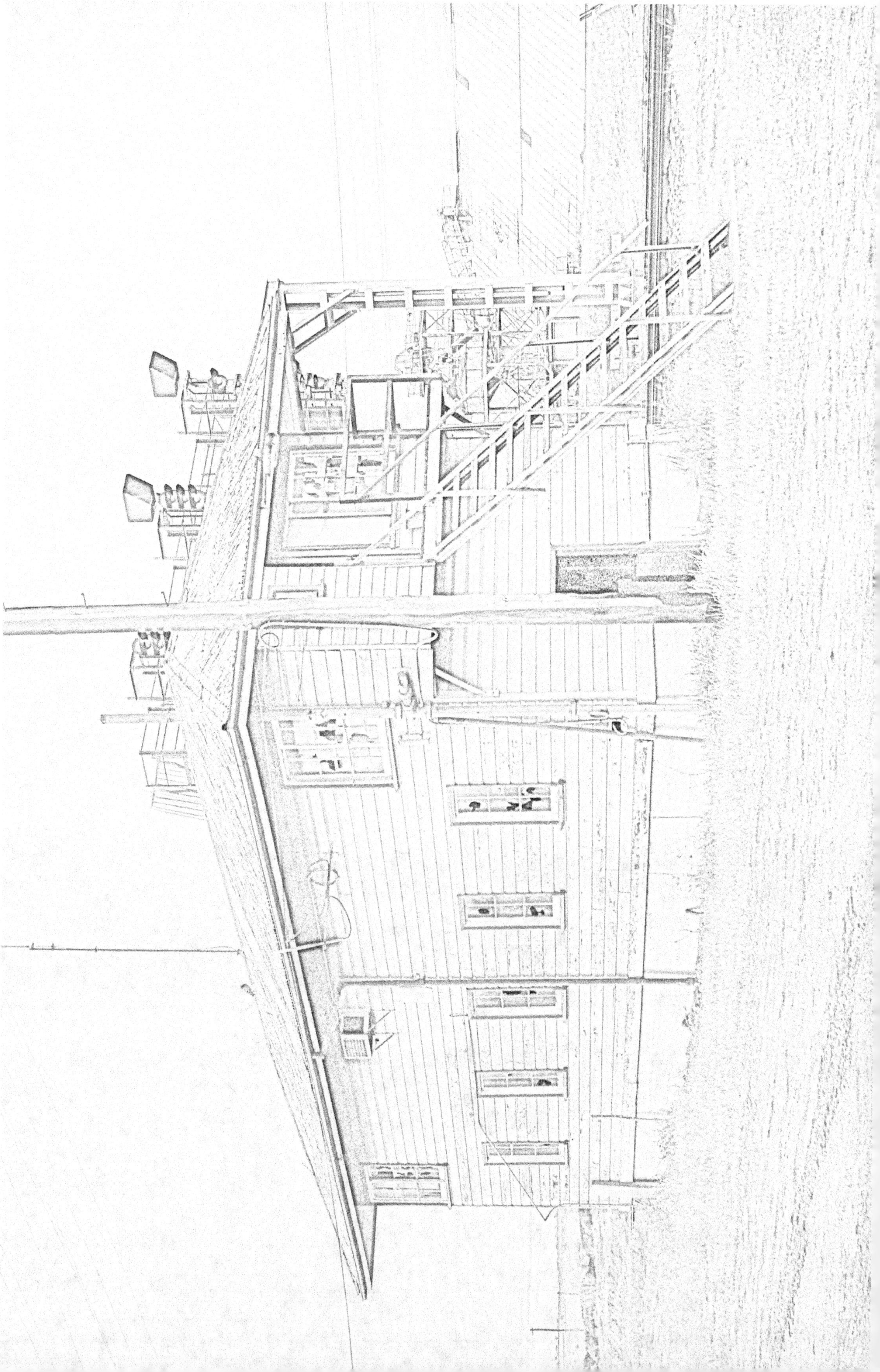

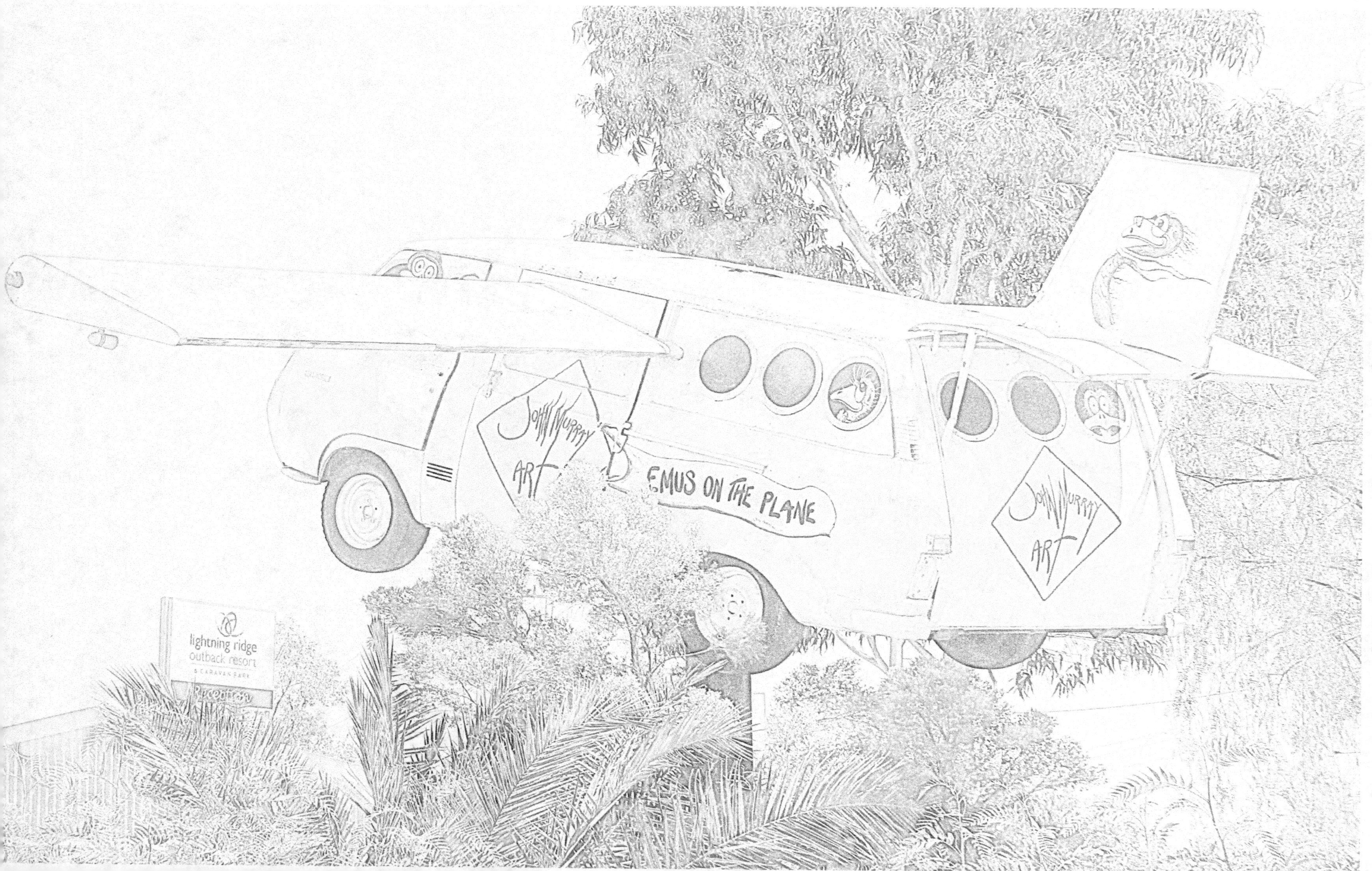
John Murray ART
EMUS ON THE PLANE
John Murray ART
lightning ridge
outback resort
& CARAVAN PARK
Reception

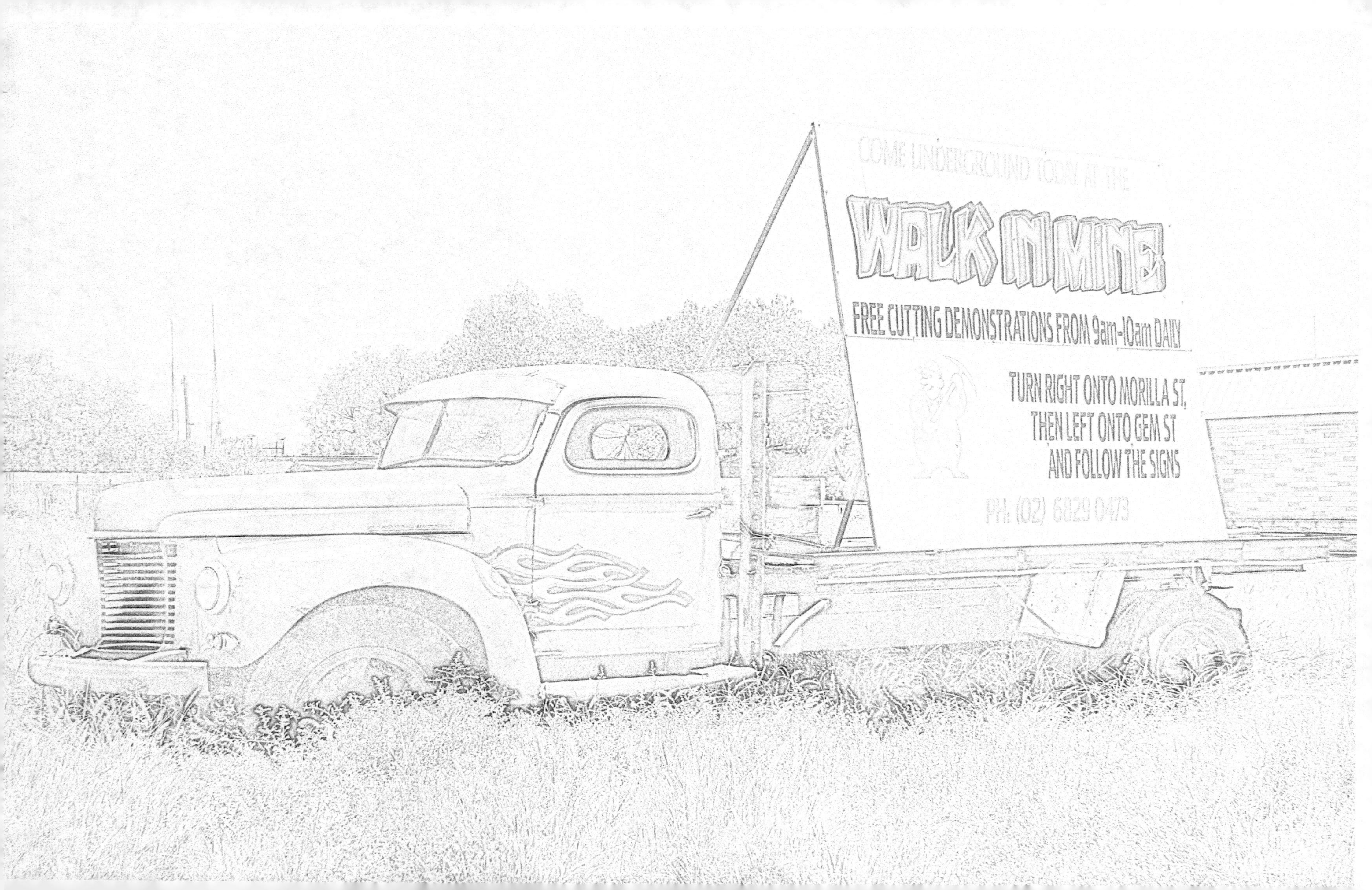
COME UNDERGROUND TODAY AT THE
WALK IN MINE
FREE CUTTING DEMONSTRATIONS FROM 9am-10am DAILY
TURN RIGHT ONTO MORILLA ST,
THEN LEFT ONTO GEM ST
AND FOLLOW THE SIGNS
PH: (02) 6829 0473

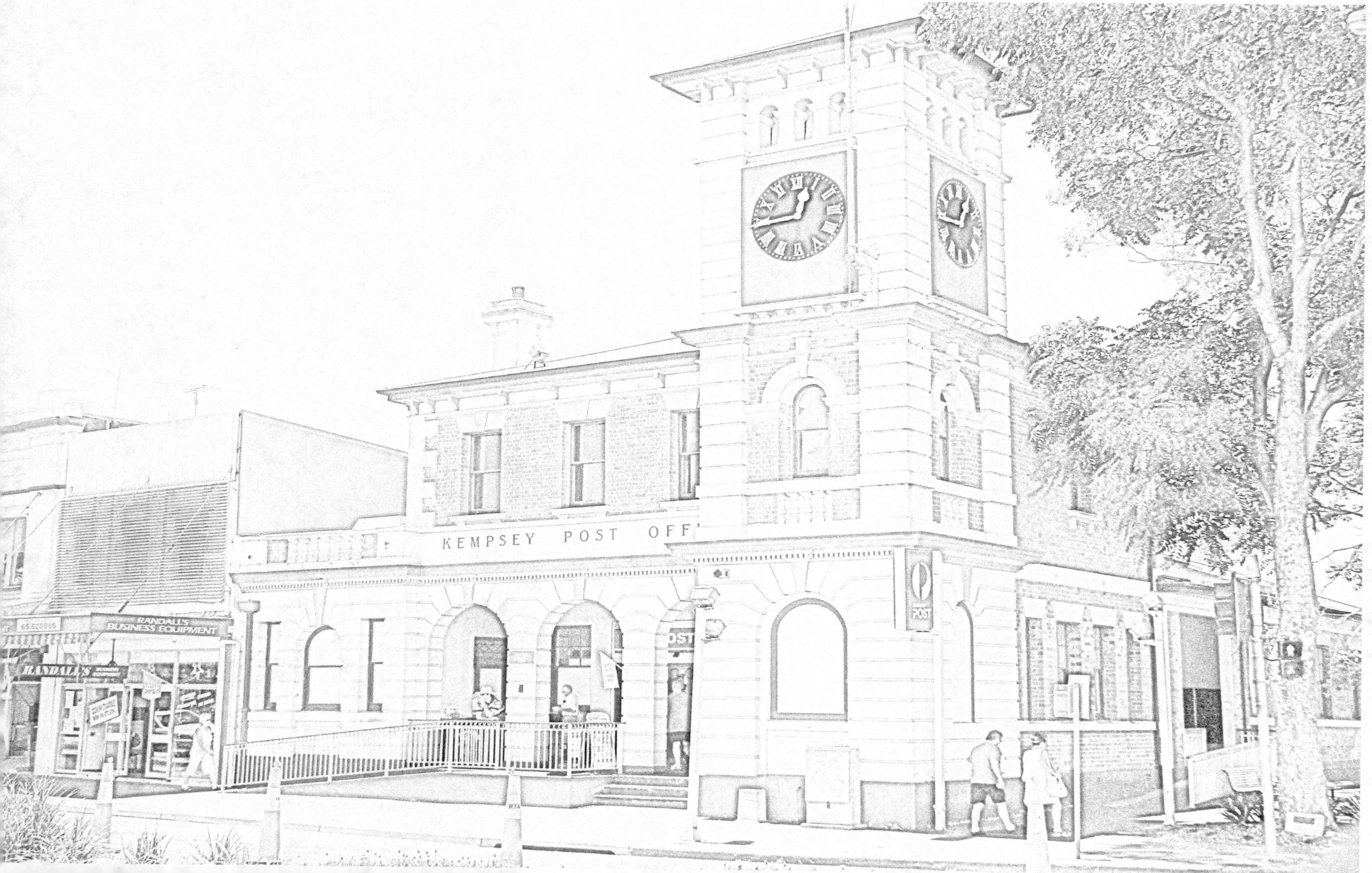
KEMPSEY POST OFF
POST
RANDALL'S BUSINESS EQUIPMENT

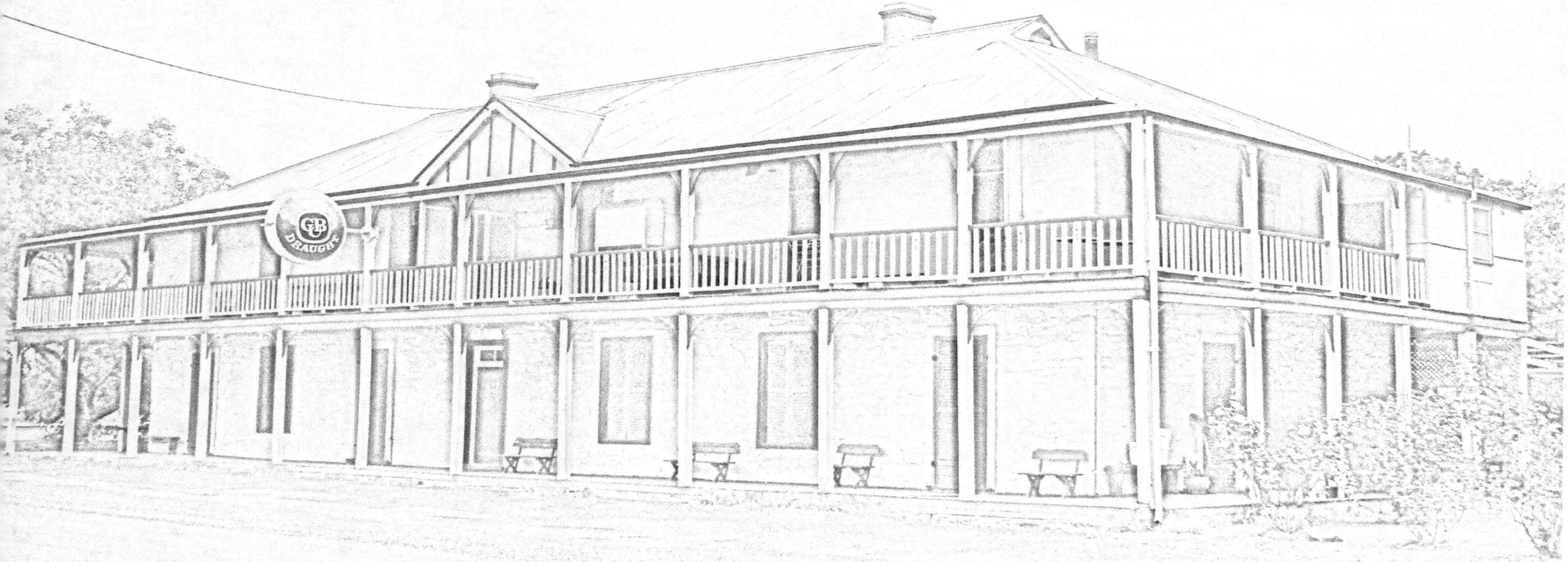
CUB
DRAUGHT

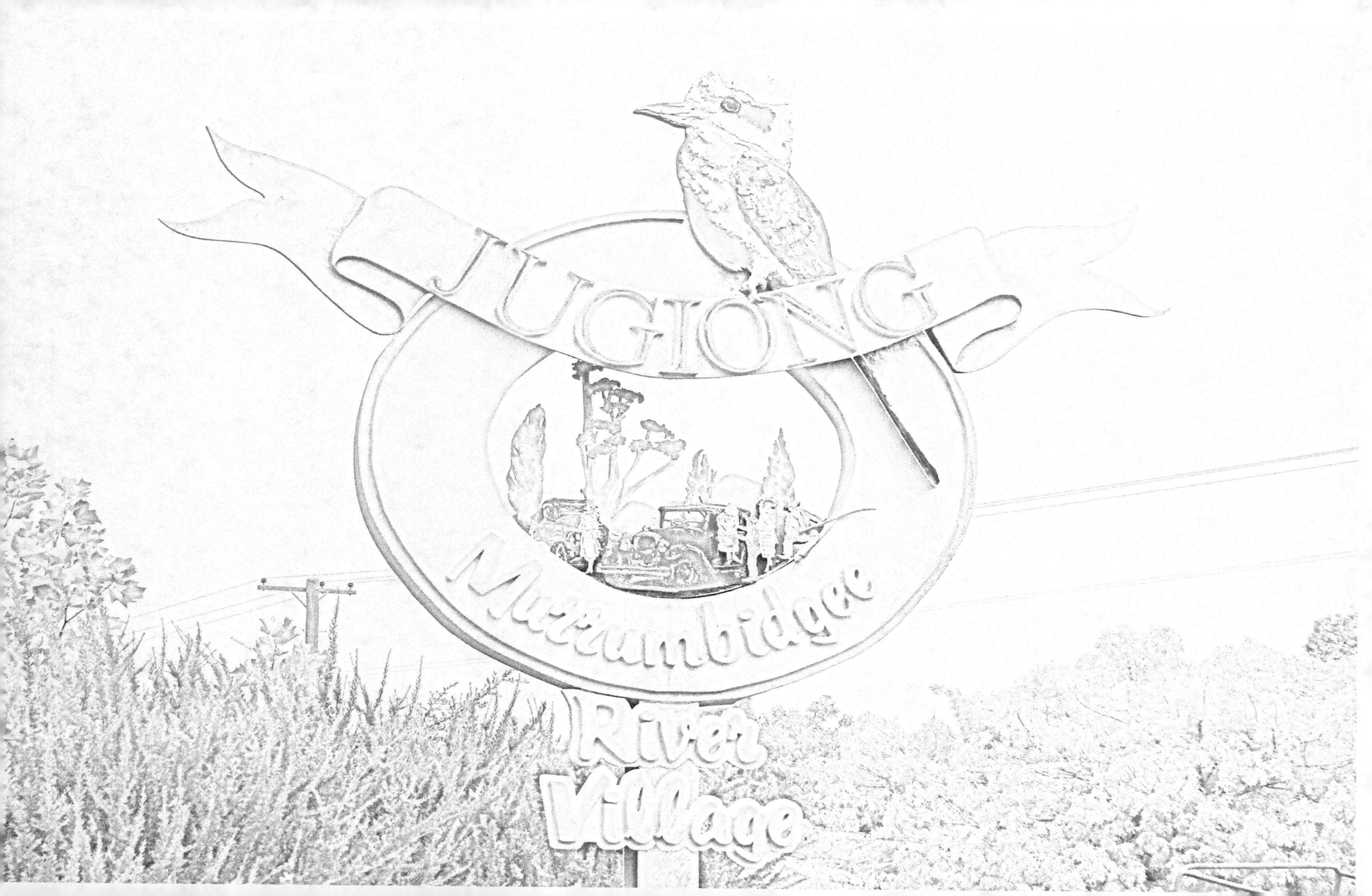
JUGIONG
Murrumbidgee
River
Village

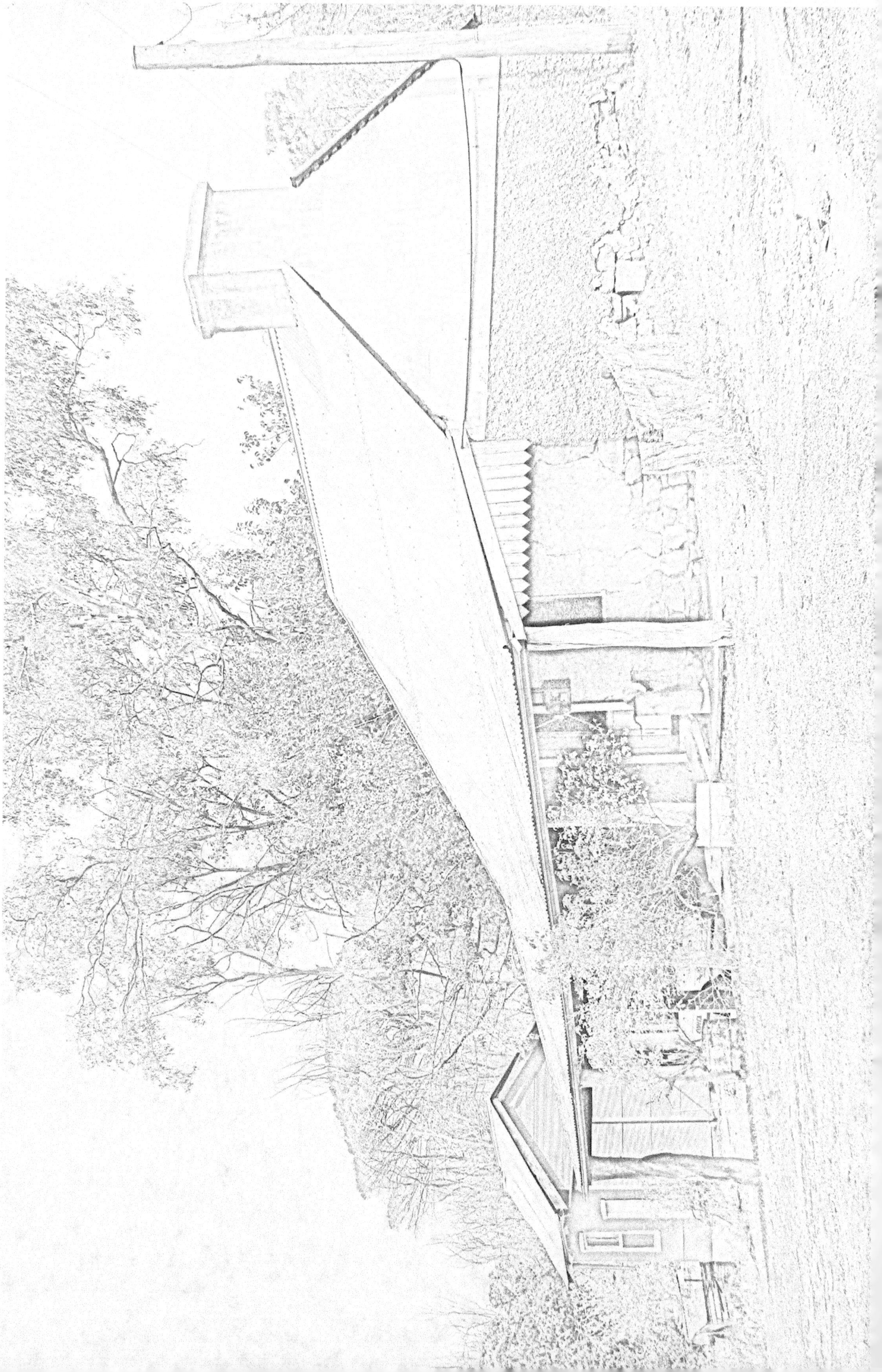

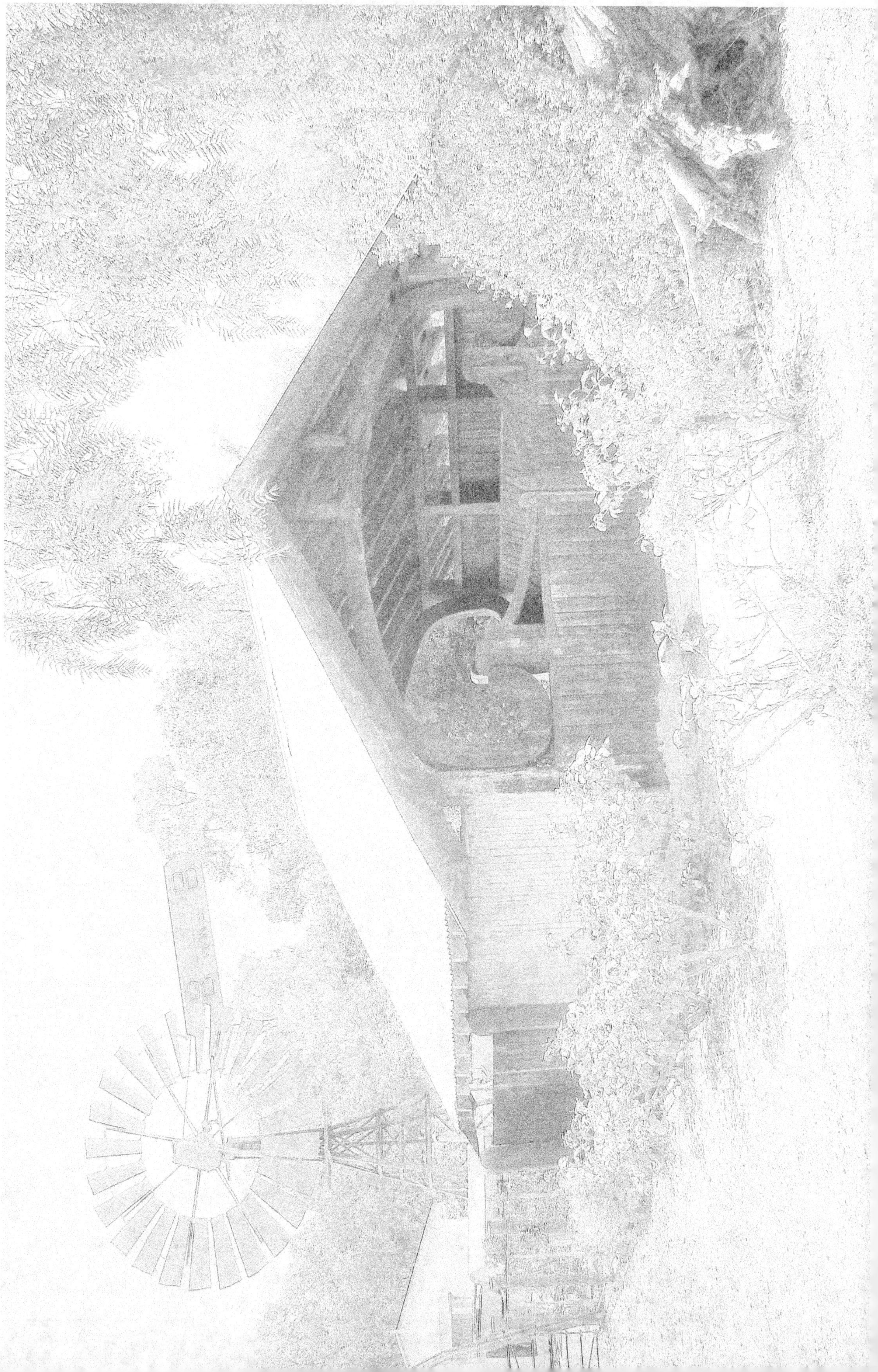

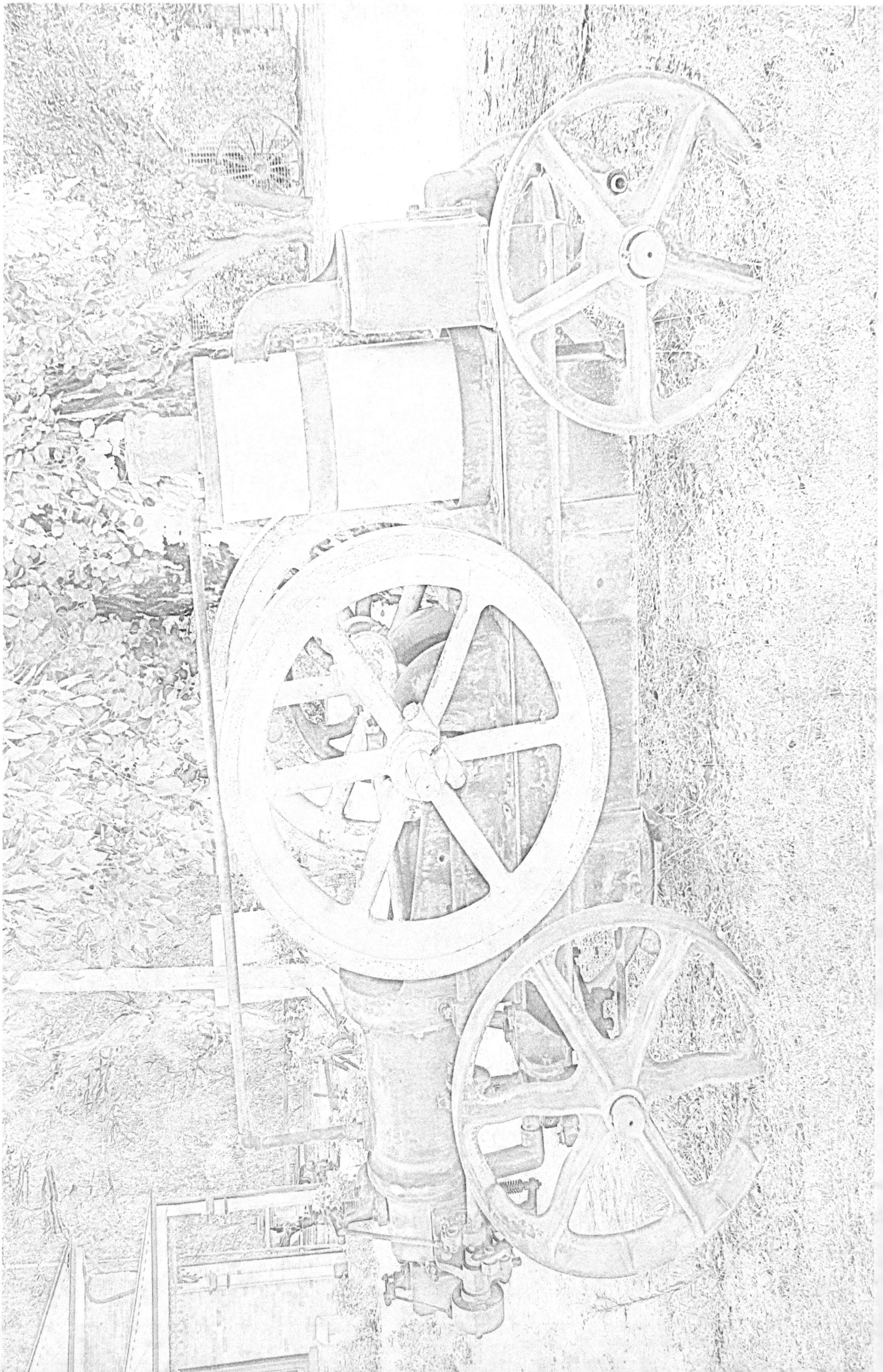

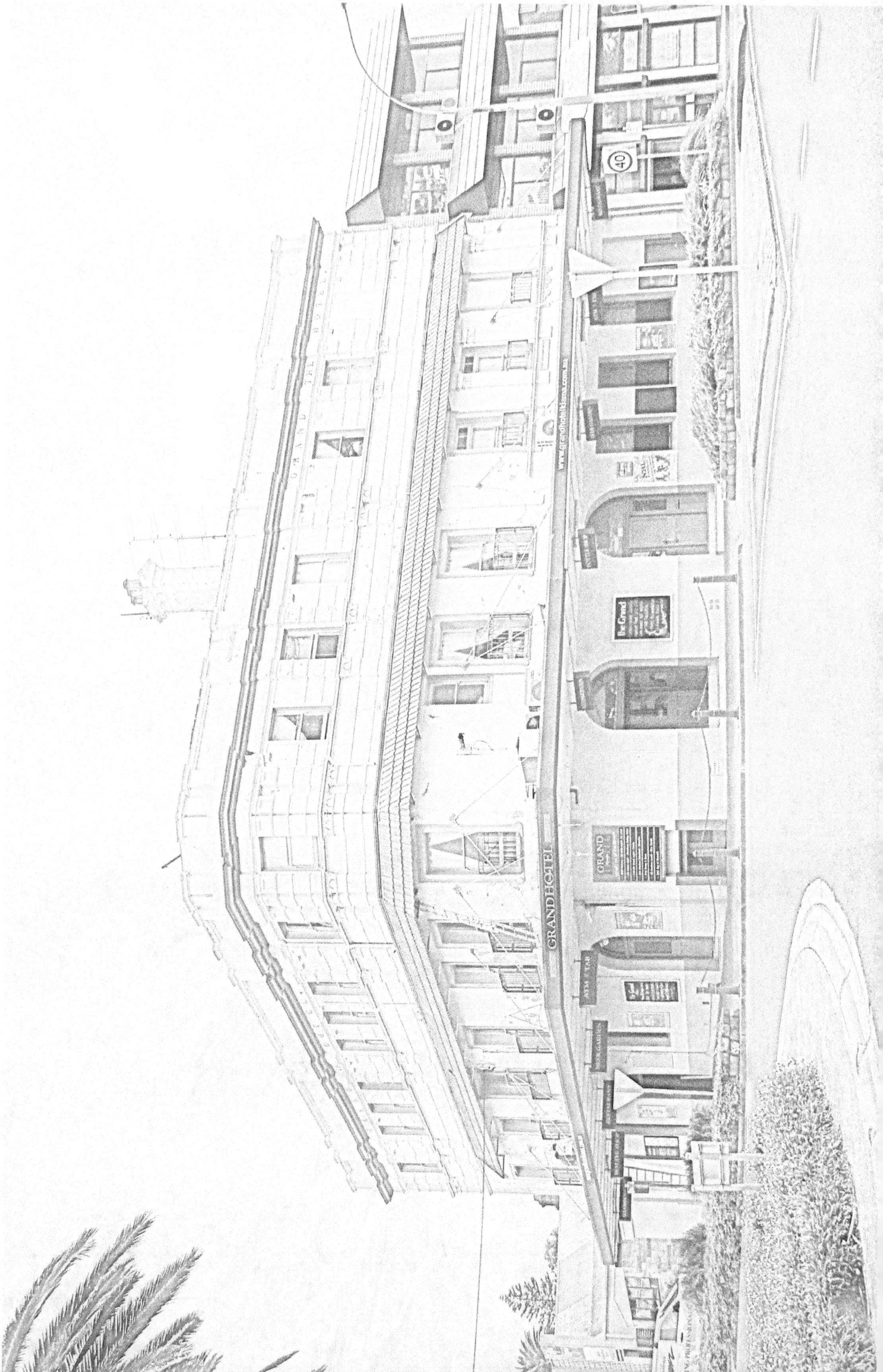
GRAND HOTEL

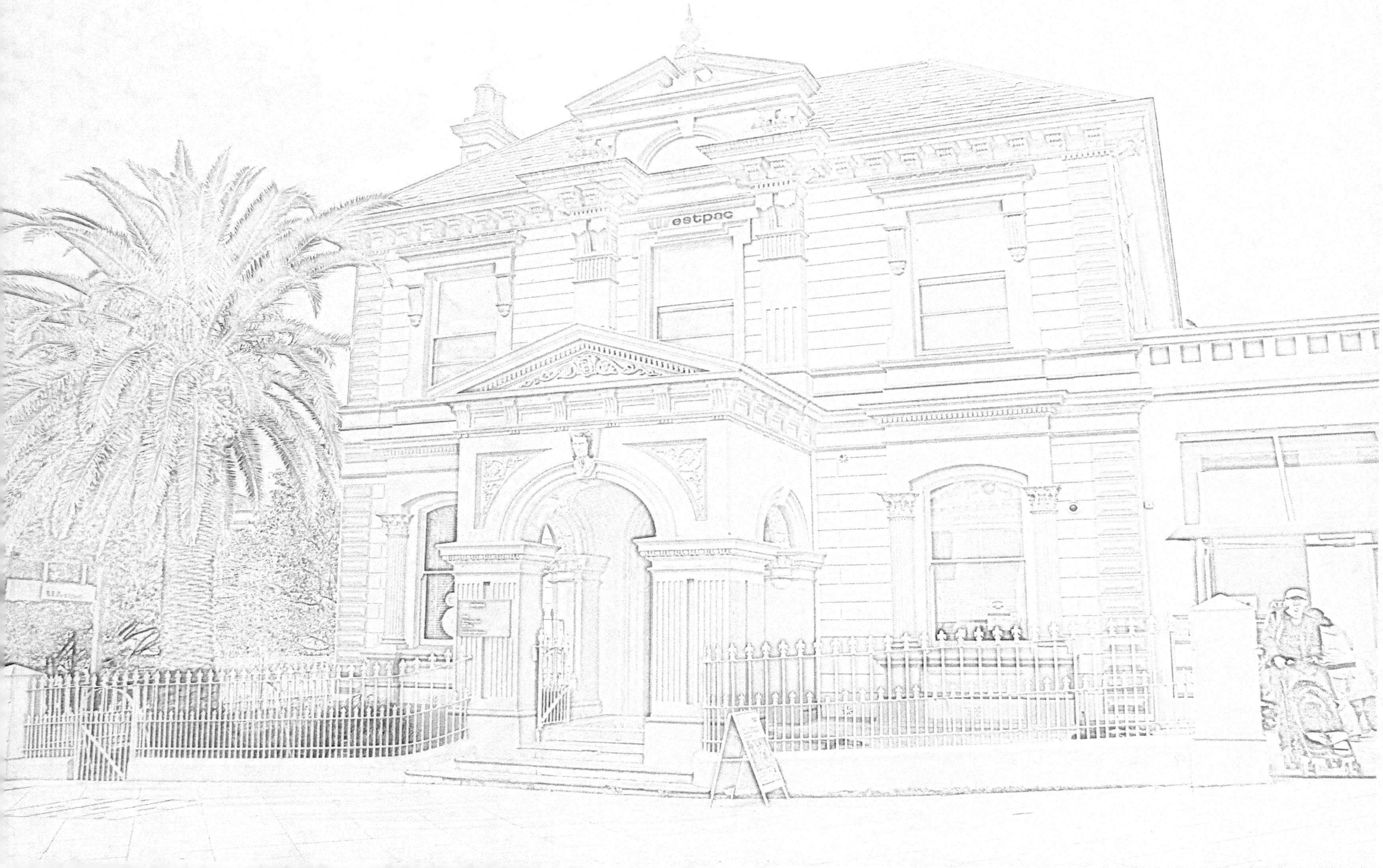
estpac

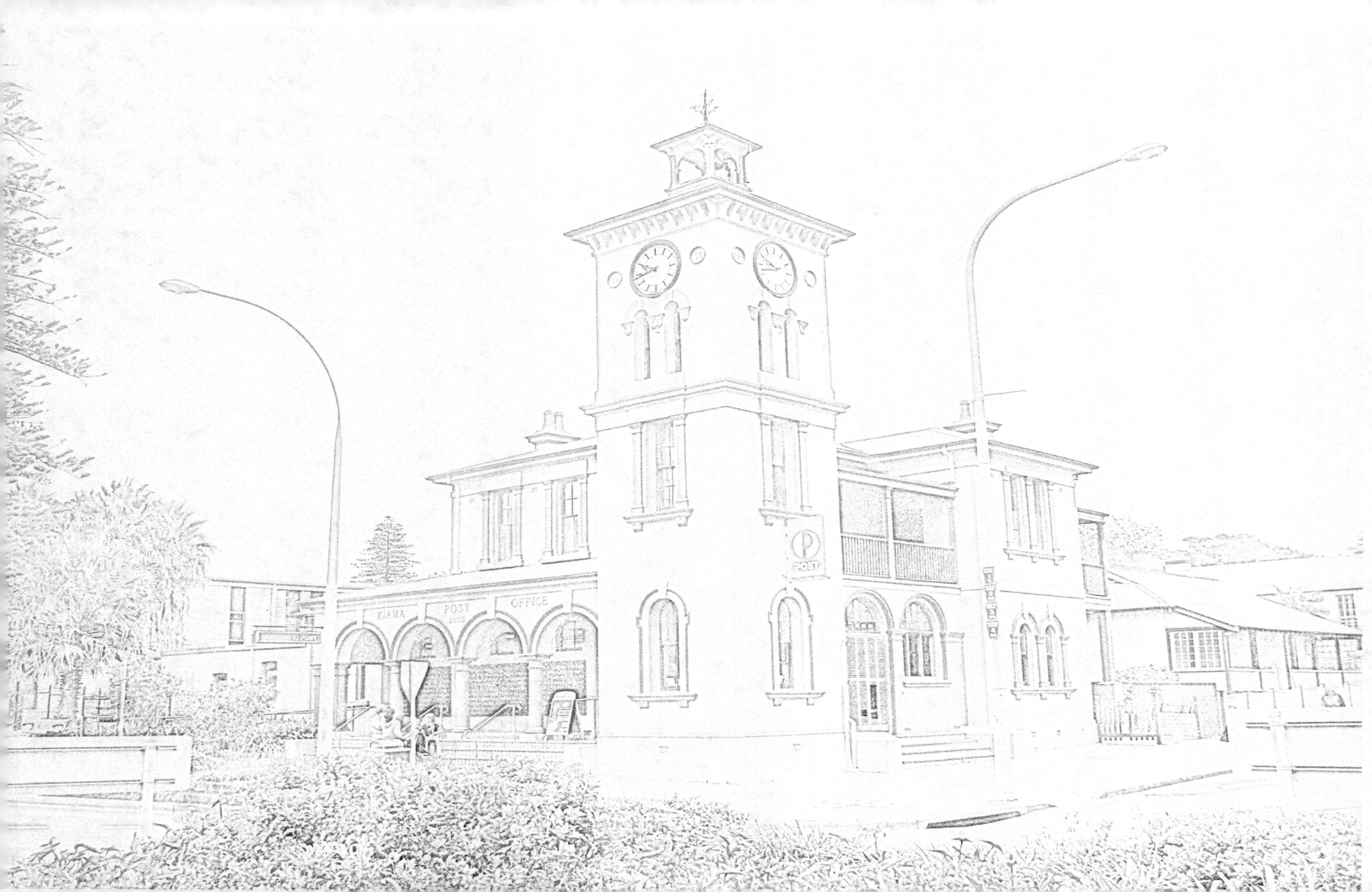

KIAMA POST OFFICE
POST

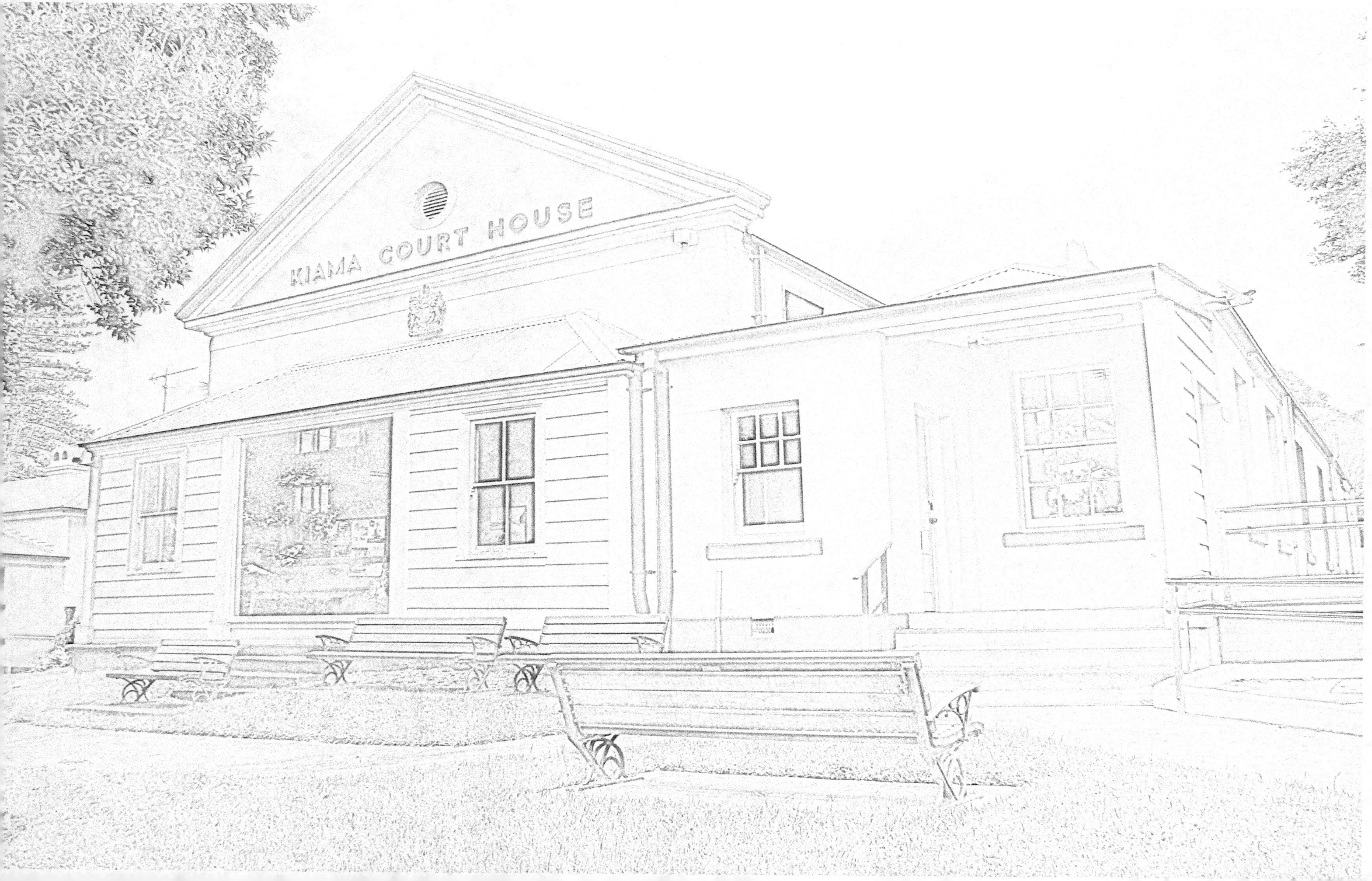
KIAMA COURT HOUSE

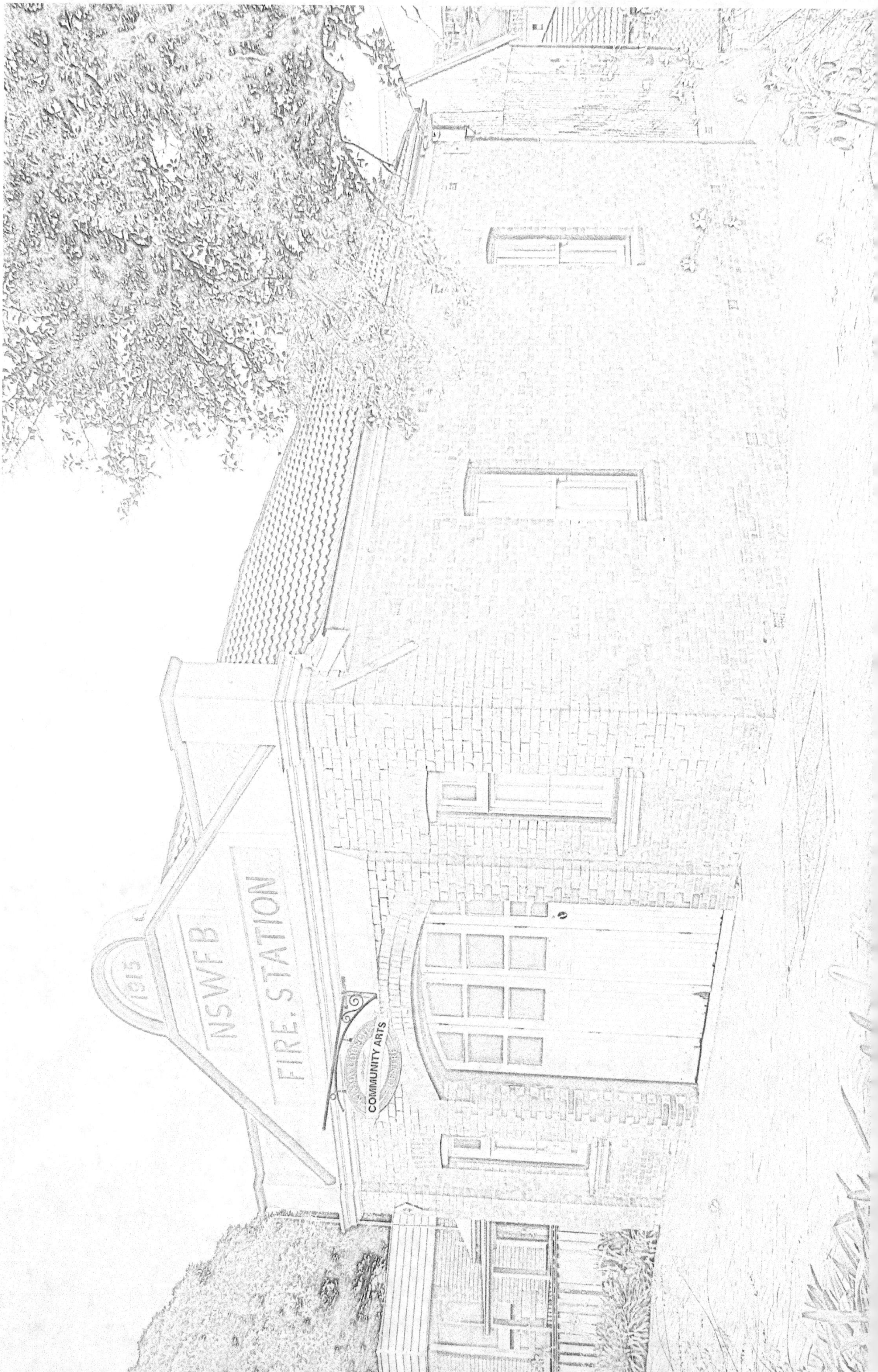
1915
NSWFB
FIRE. STATION
COMMUNITY ARTS

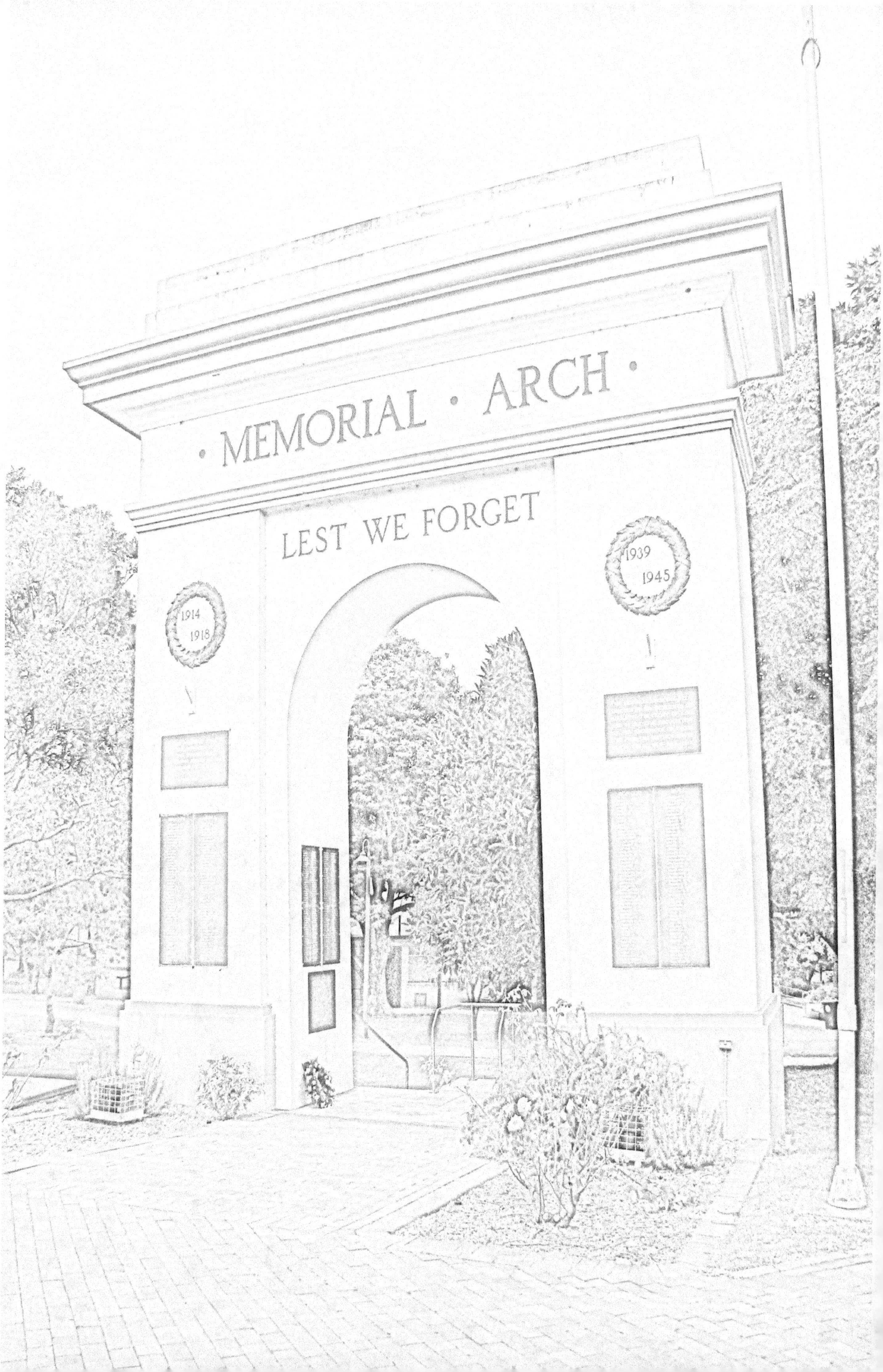

• MEMORIAL • ARCH •
LEST WE FORGET
1914
1918
1939
1945

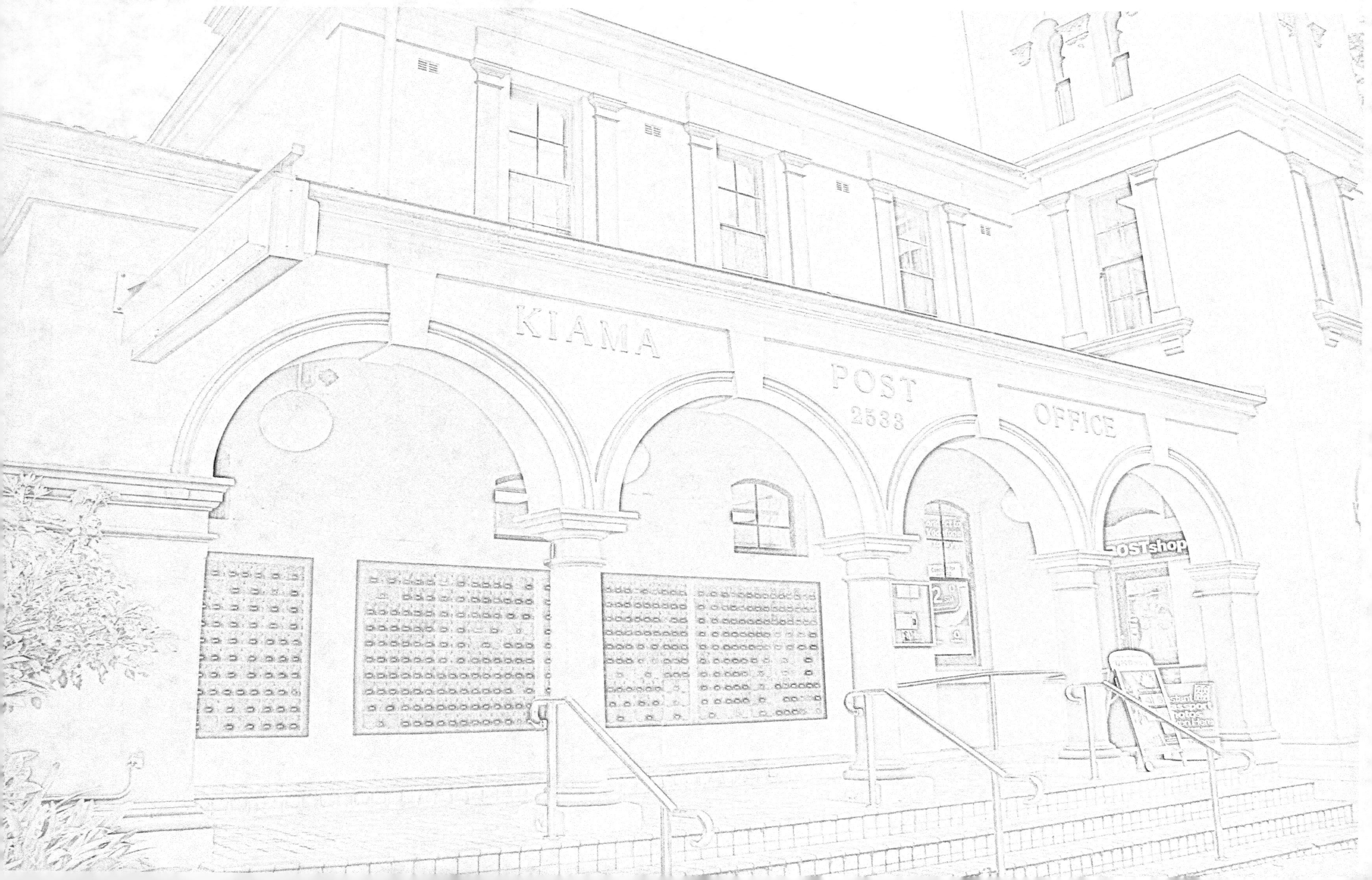
KIAMA POST OFFICE
2533

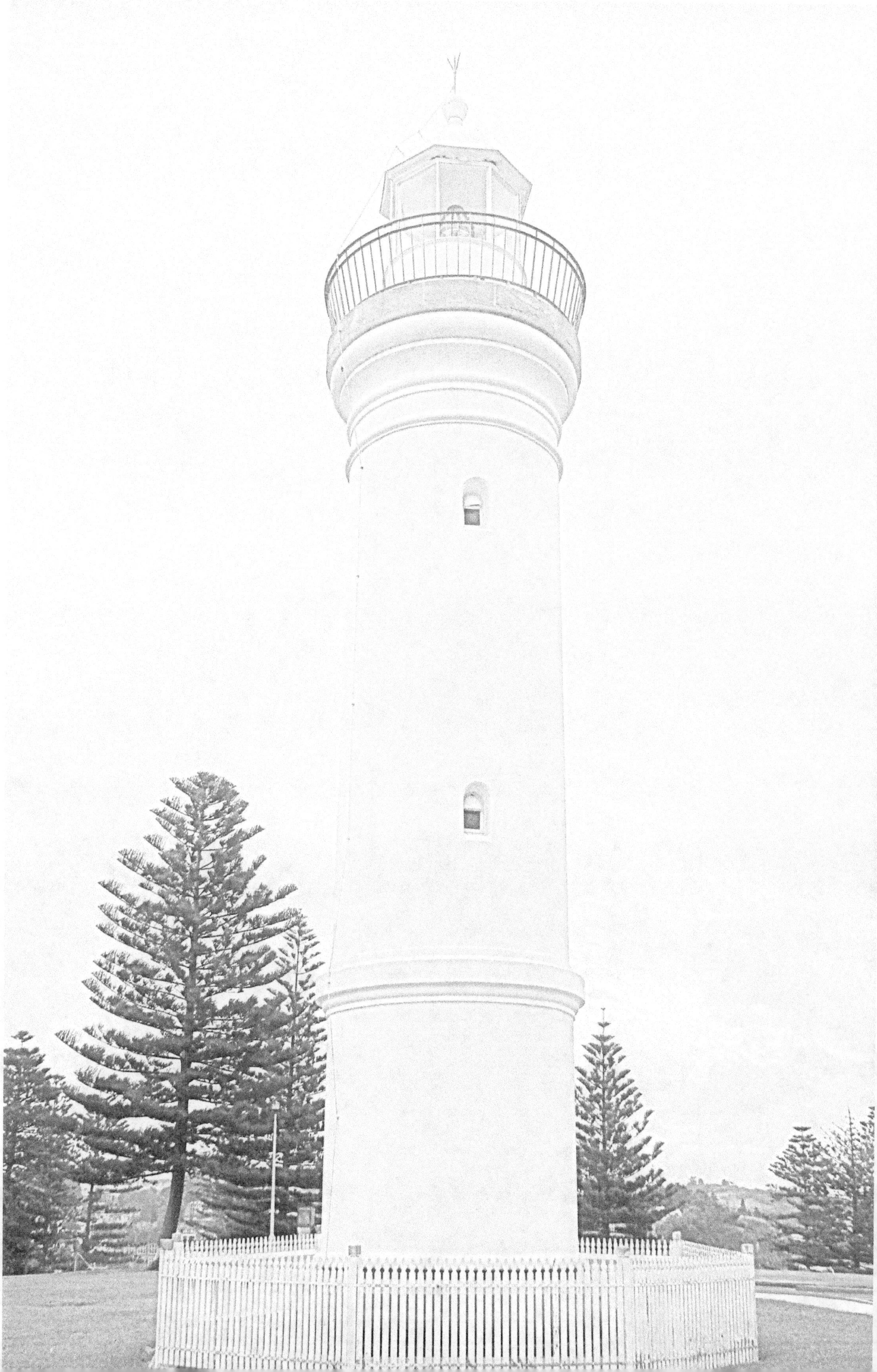

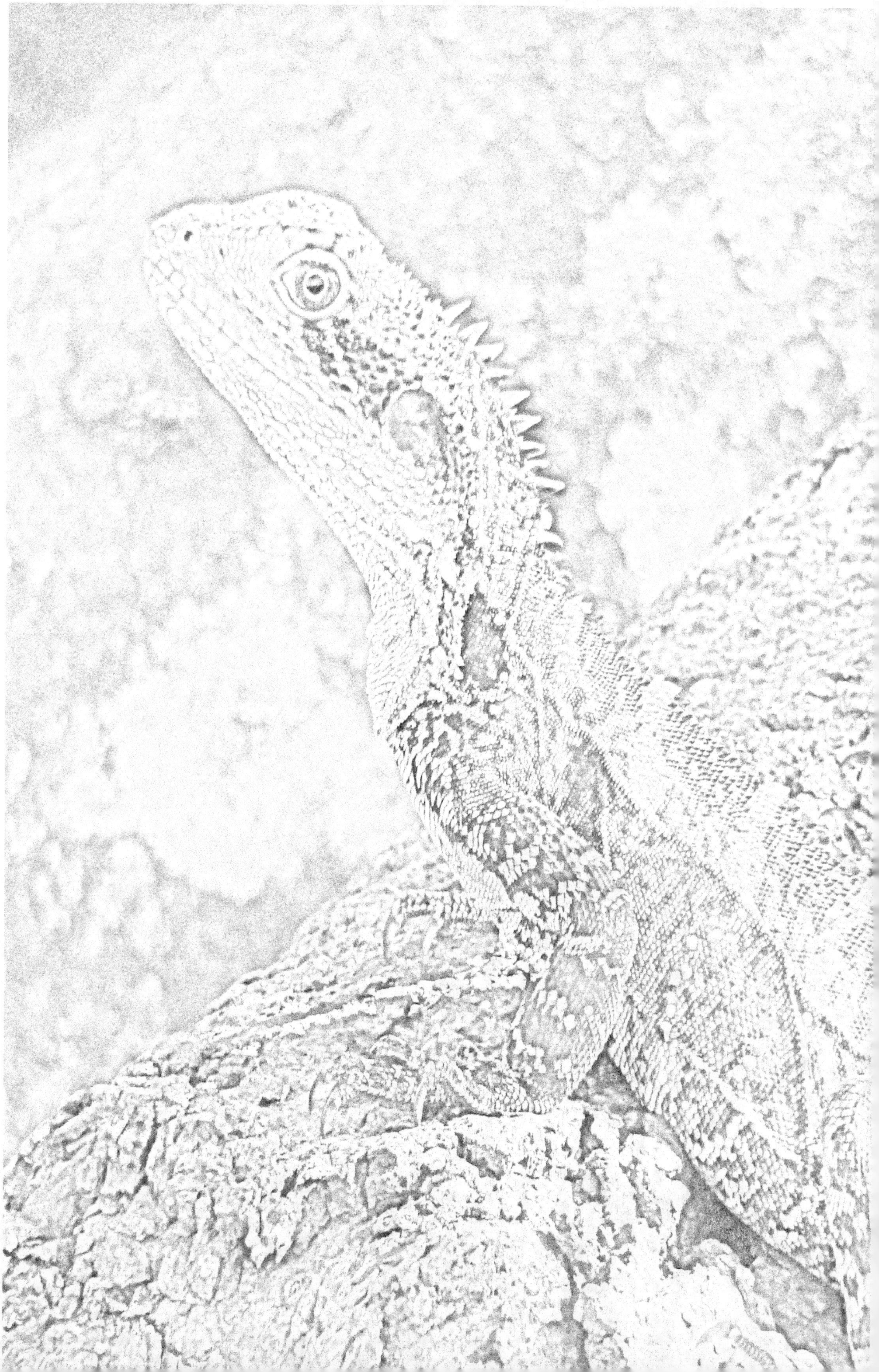

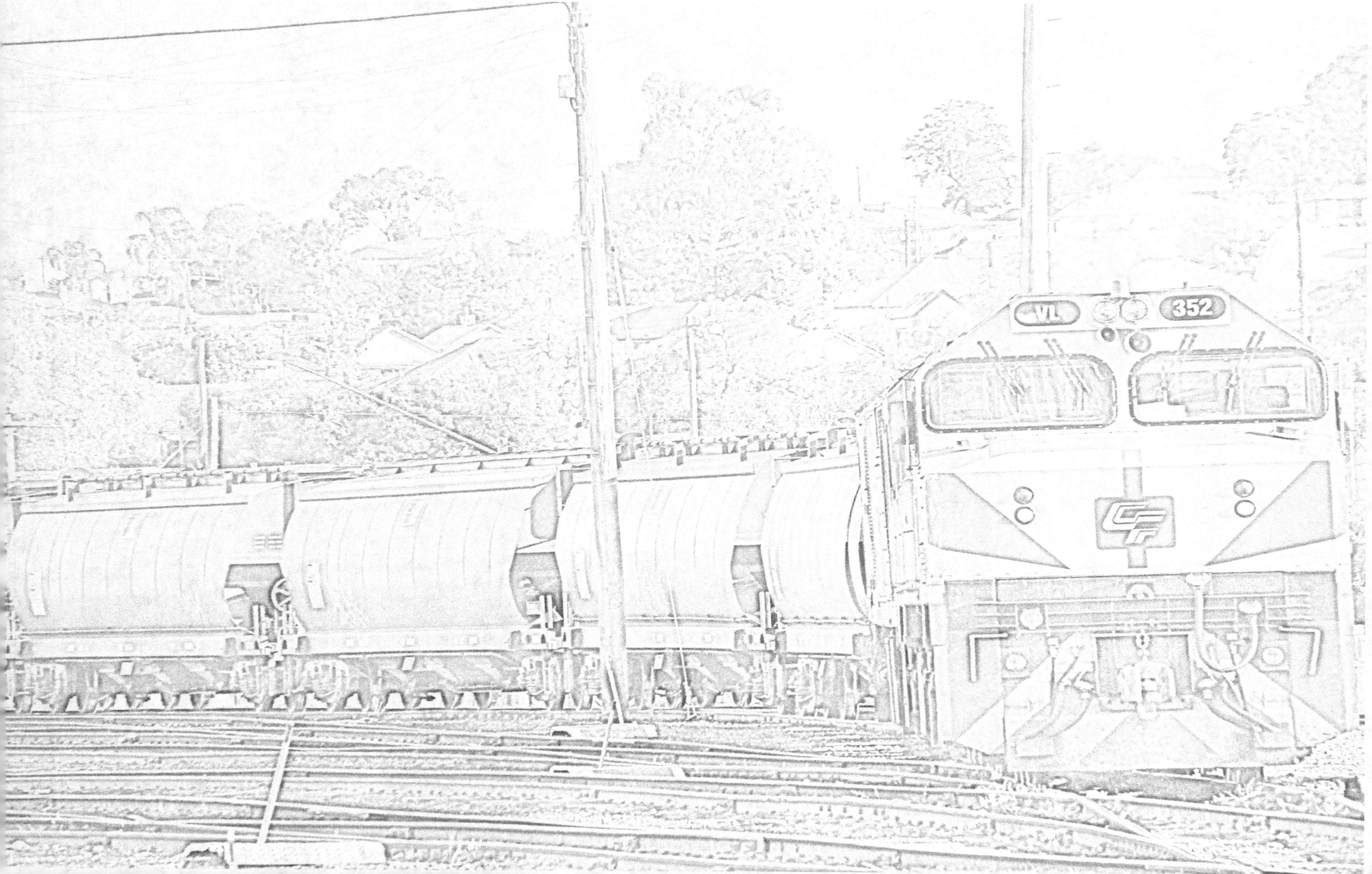
VL
352

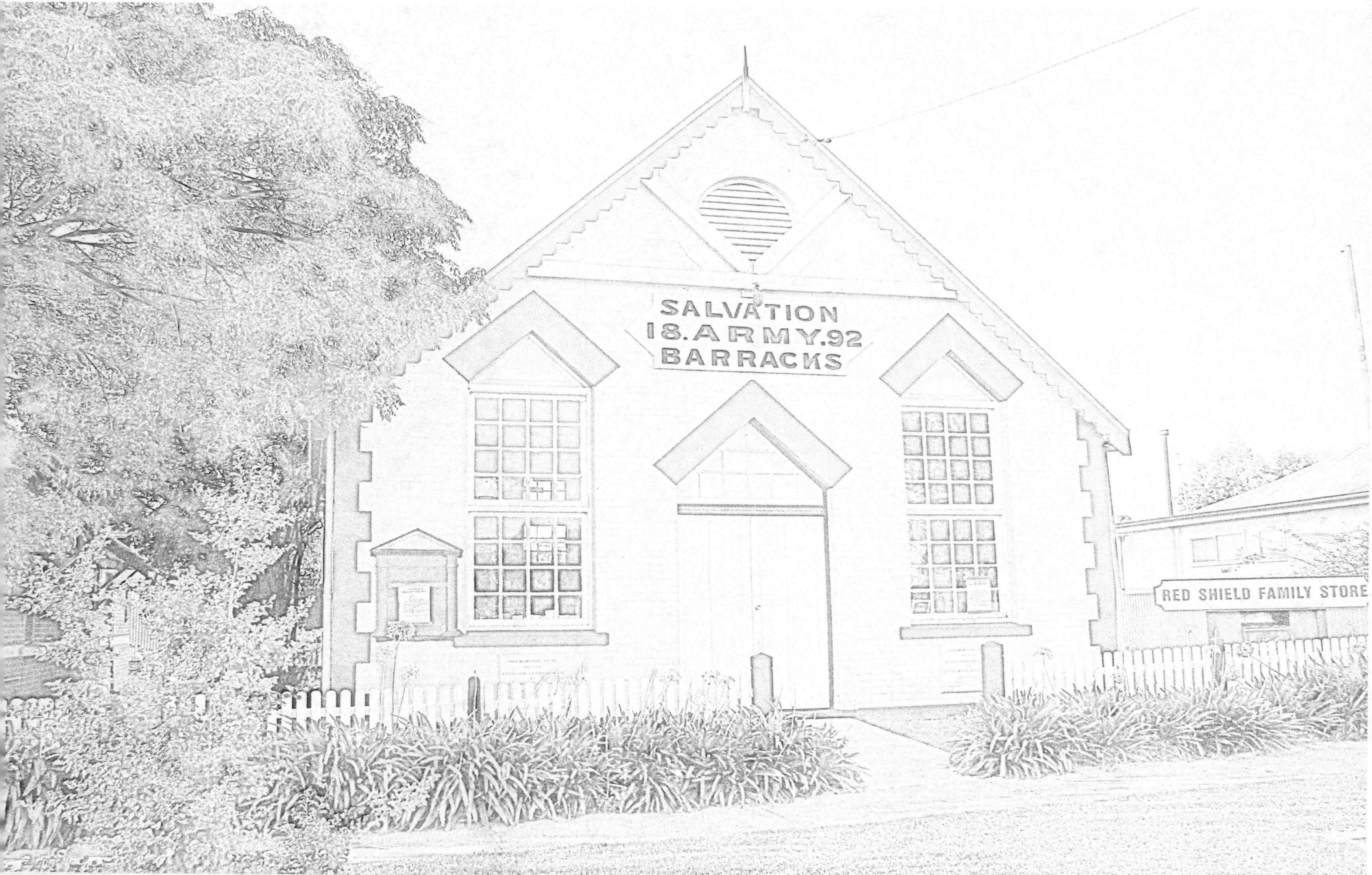
SALVATION
18. ARMY. 92
BARRACKS
RED SHIELD FAMILY STORE

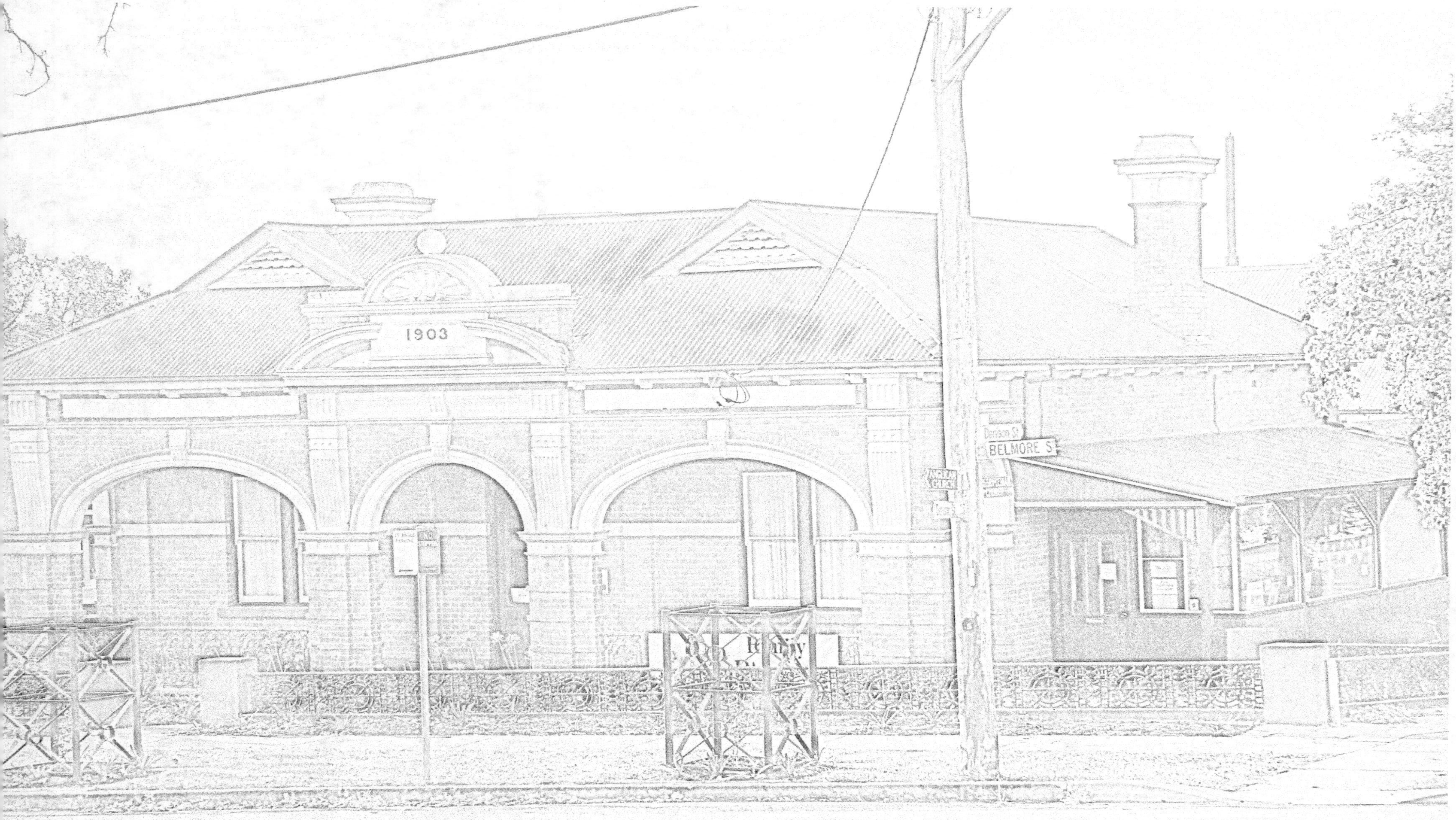
1903
Denison St
BELMORE S
ANGLICAN CHURCH

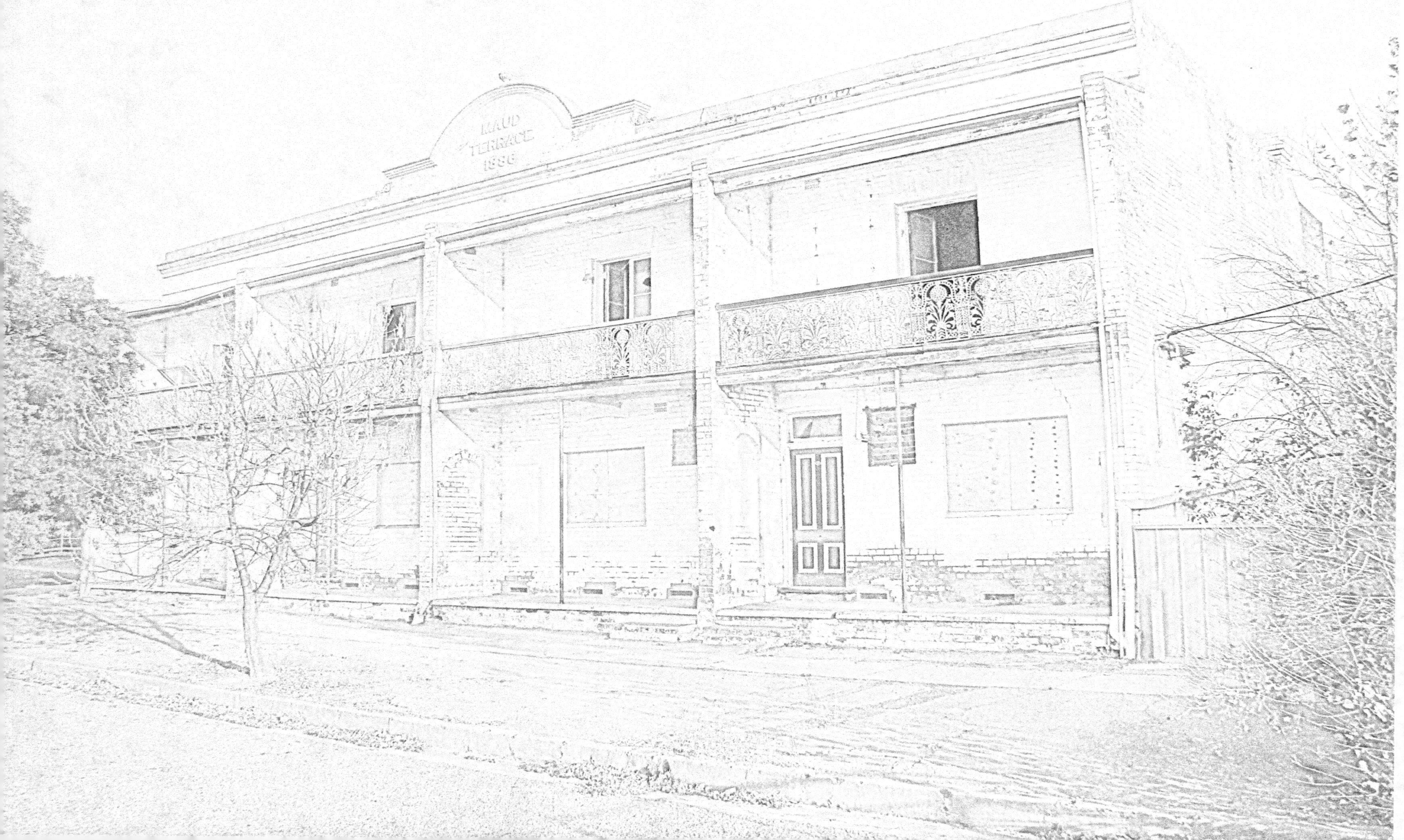
MAUD
TERRACE
1886

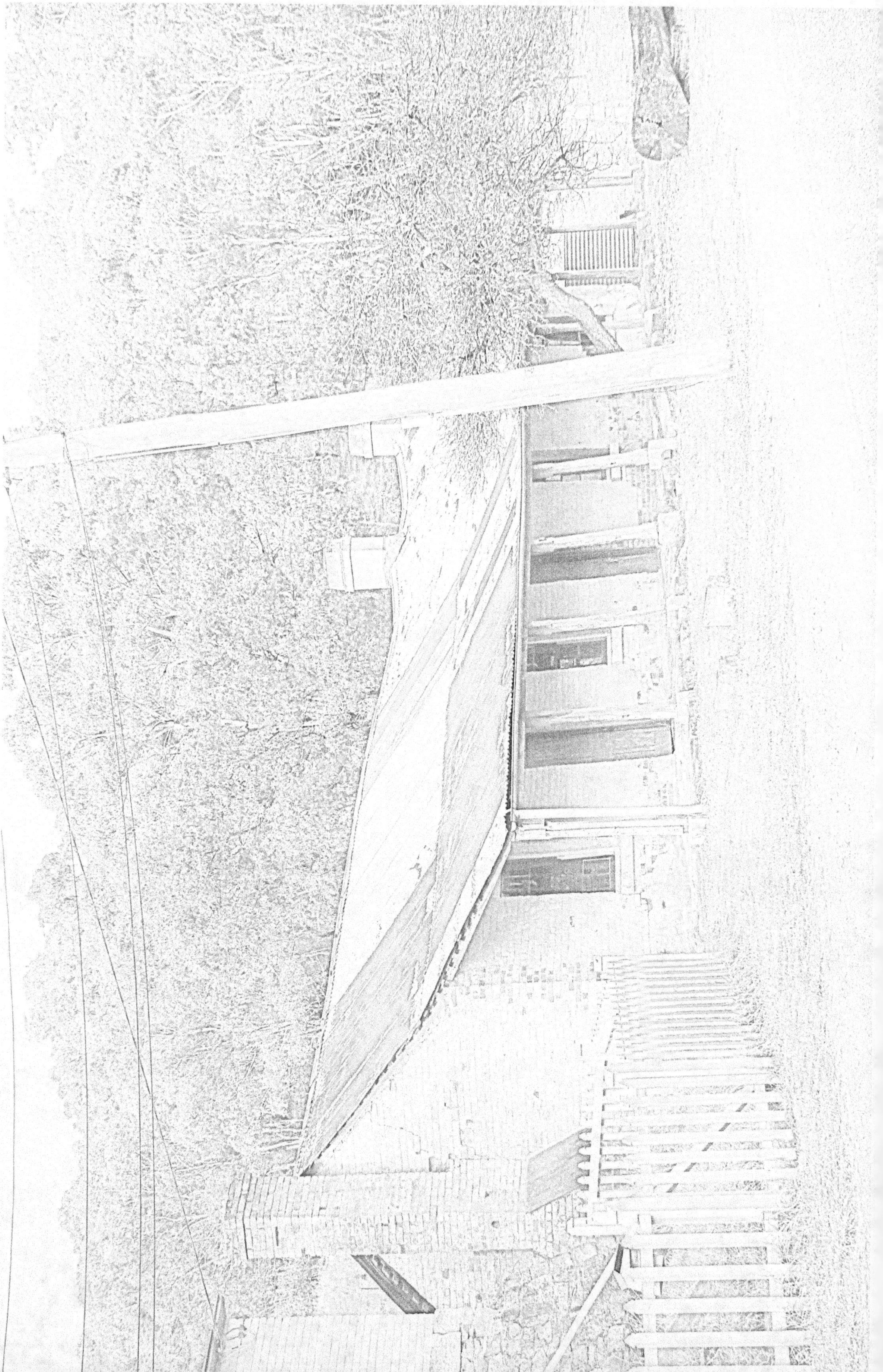

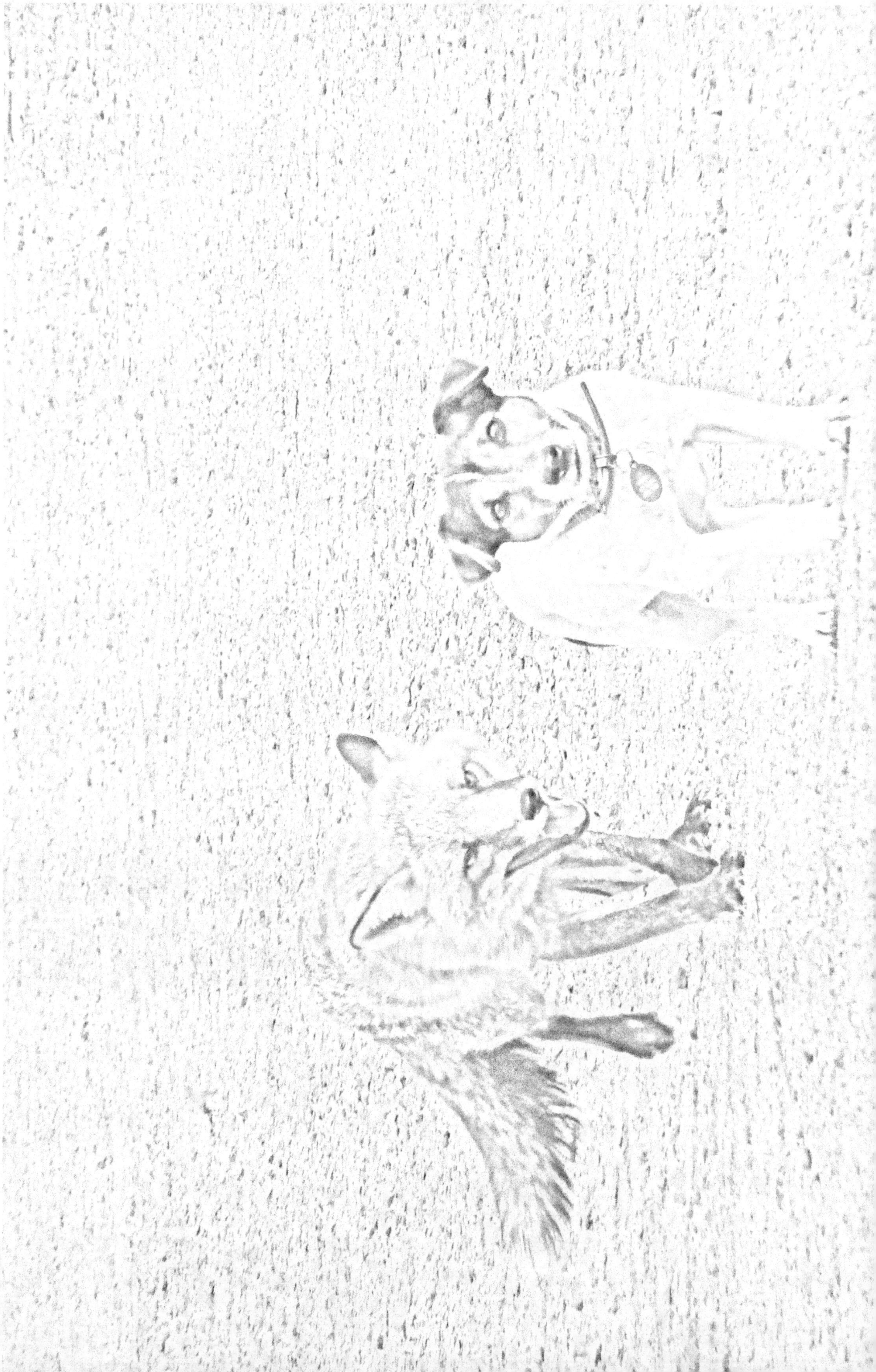

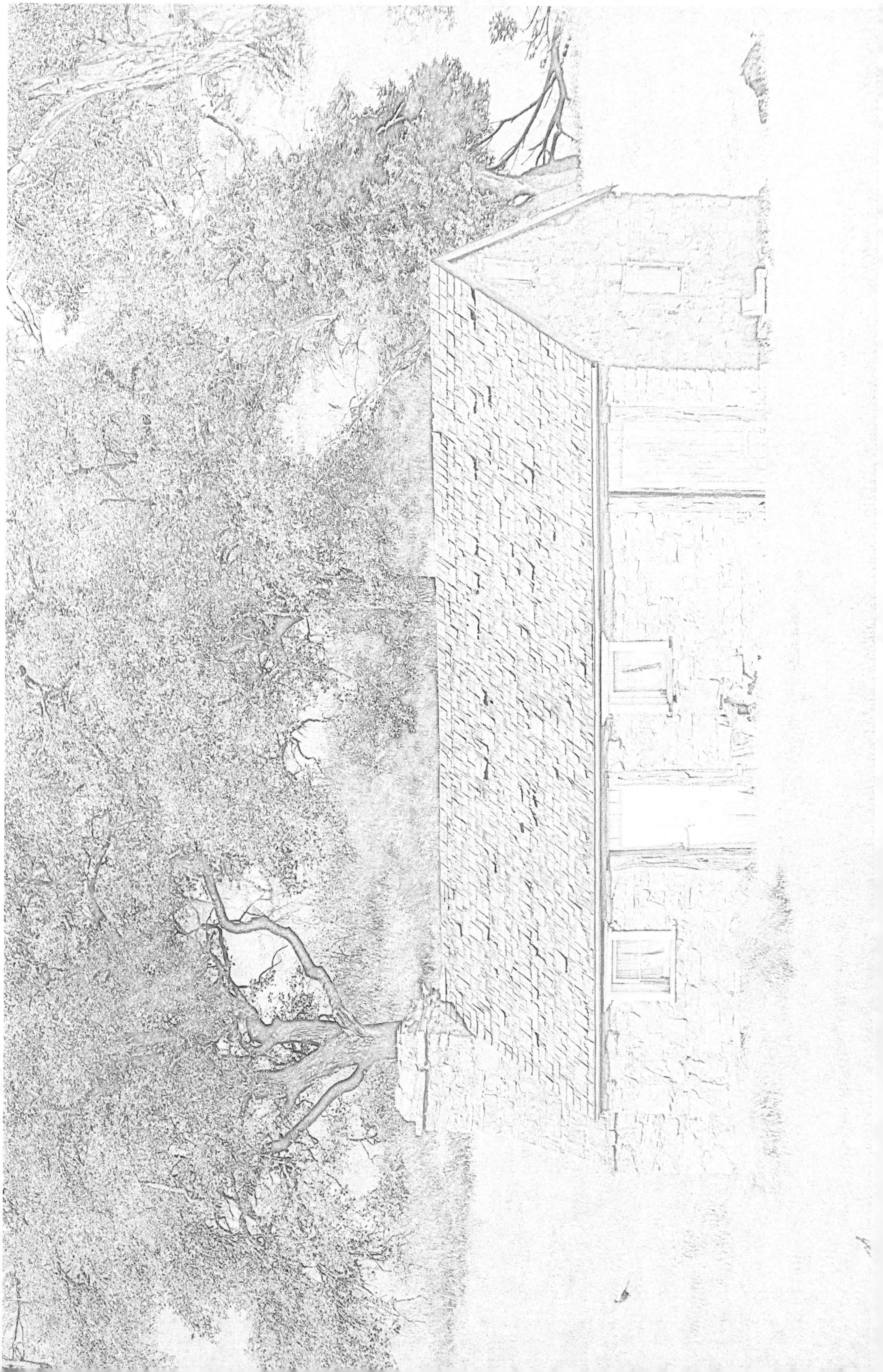

UNITING CHURCH
HILLGROVE

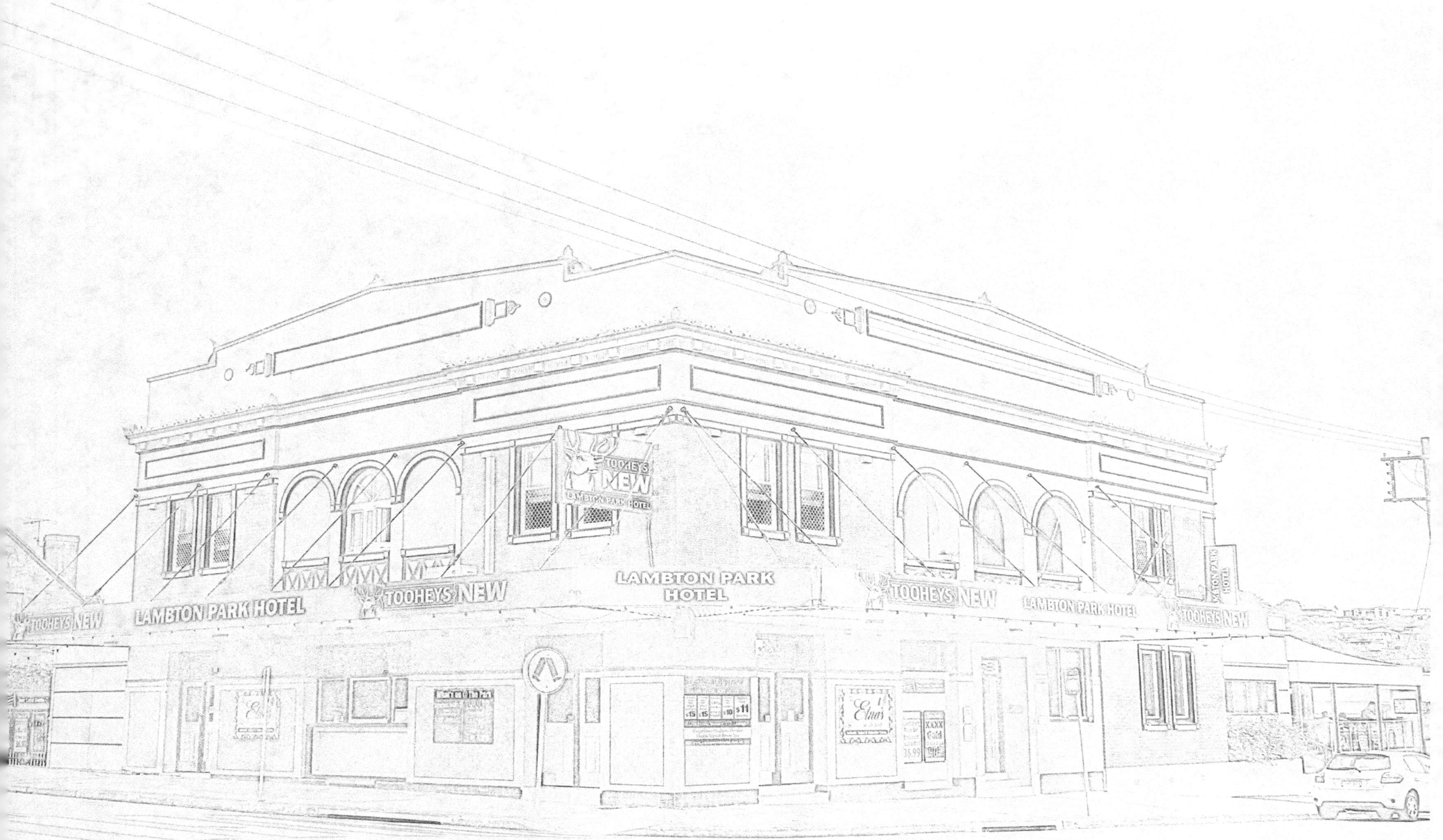
TOOHEYS NEW
LAMBTON PARK HOTEL
TOOHEYS NEW
TOOHEYS NEW
LAMBTON PARK HOTEL
LAMBTON PARK
HOTEL
TOOHEYS NEW
LAMBTON PARK HOTEL
TOOHEYS NEW

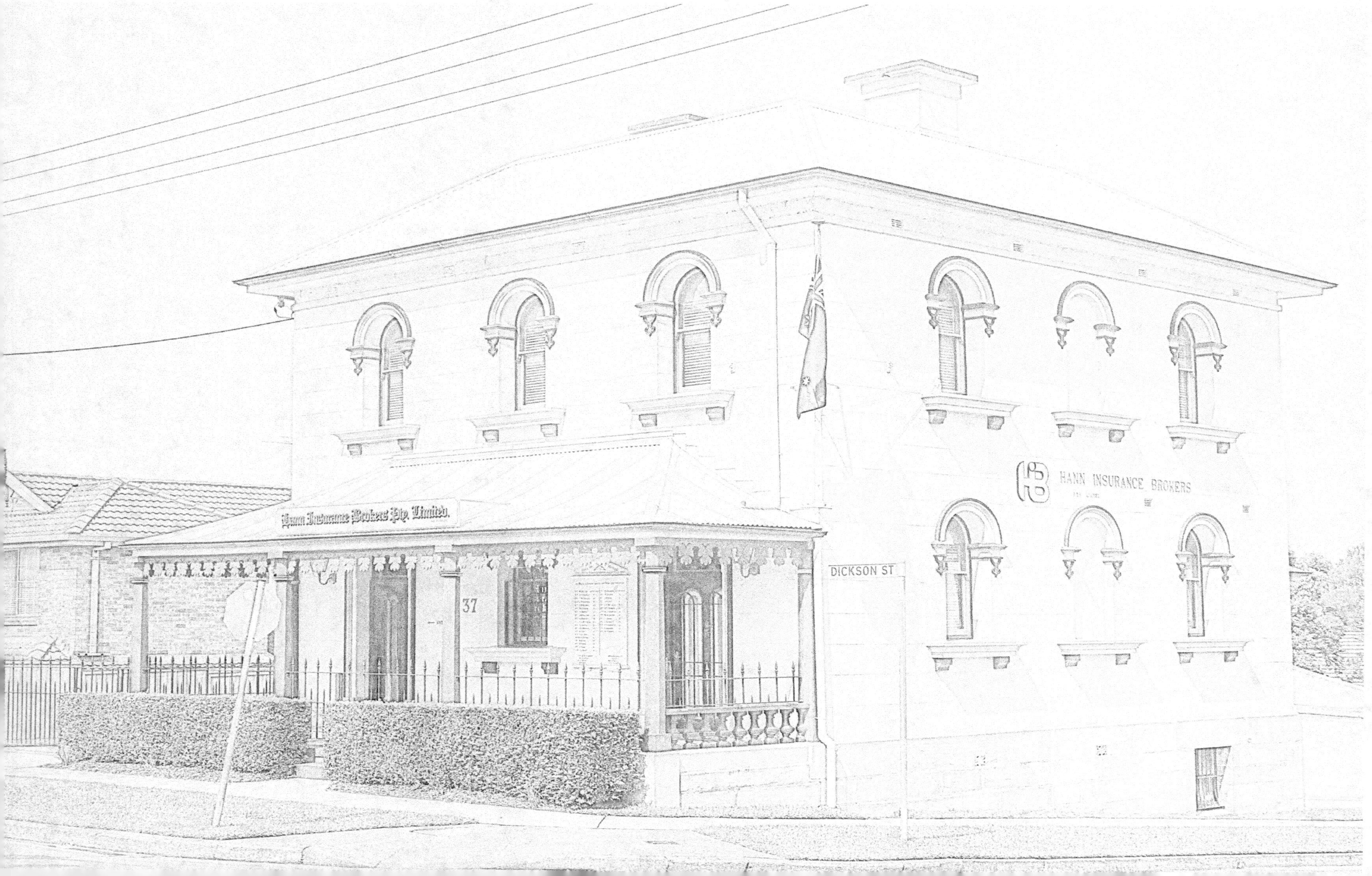
Hann Insurance Brokers Pty. Limited.
37
DICKSON ST
HANN INSURANCE BROKERS

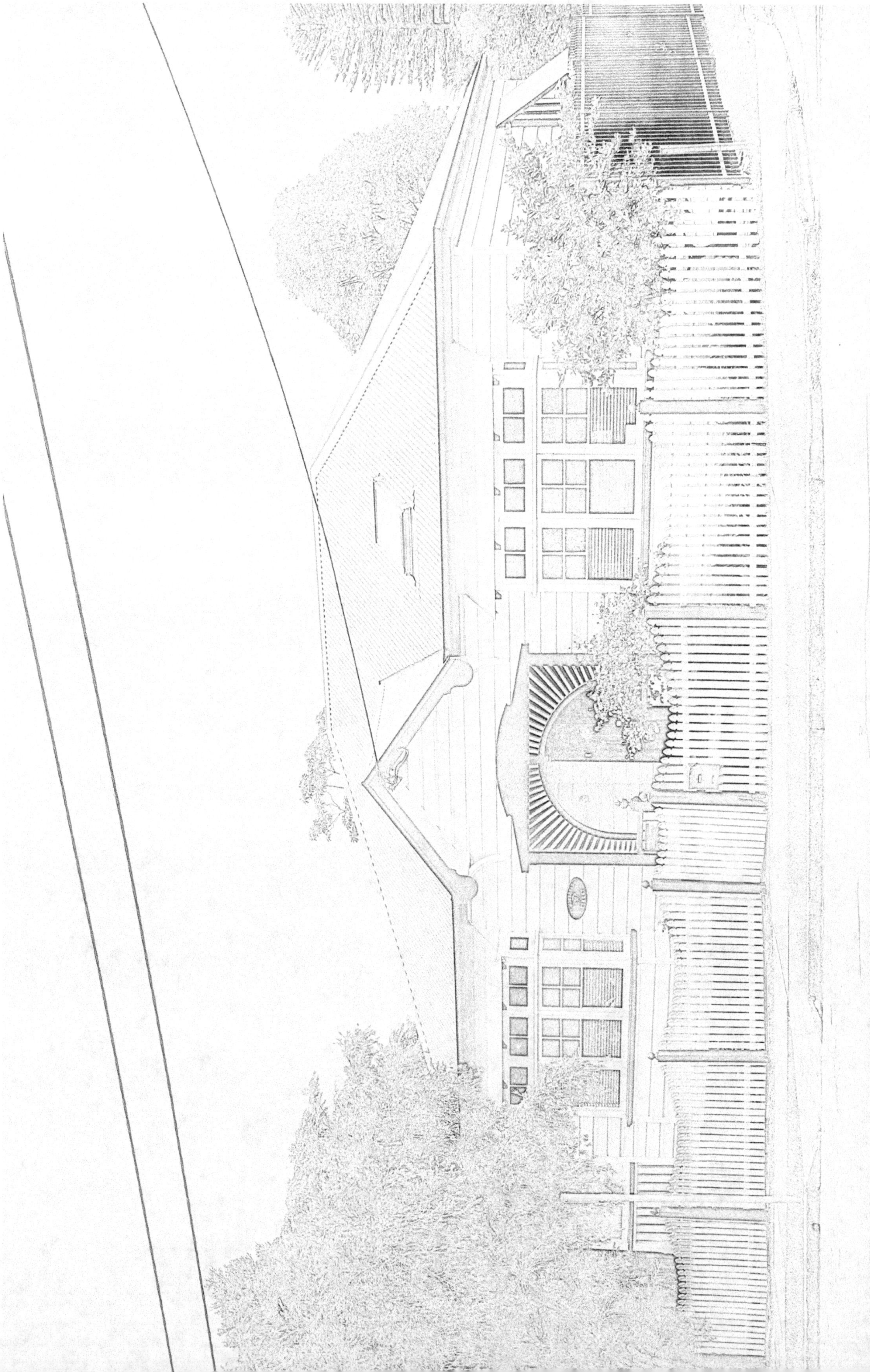

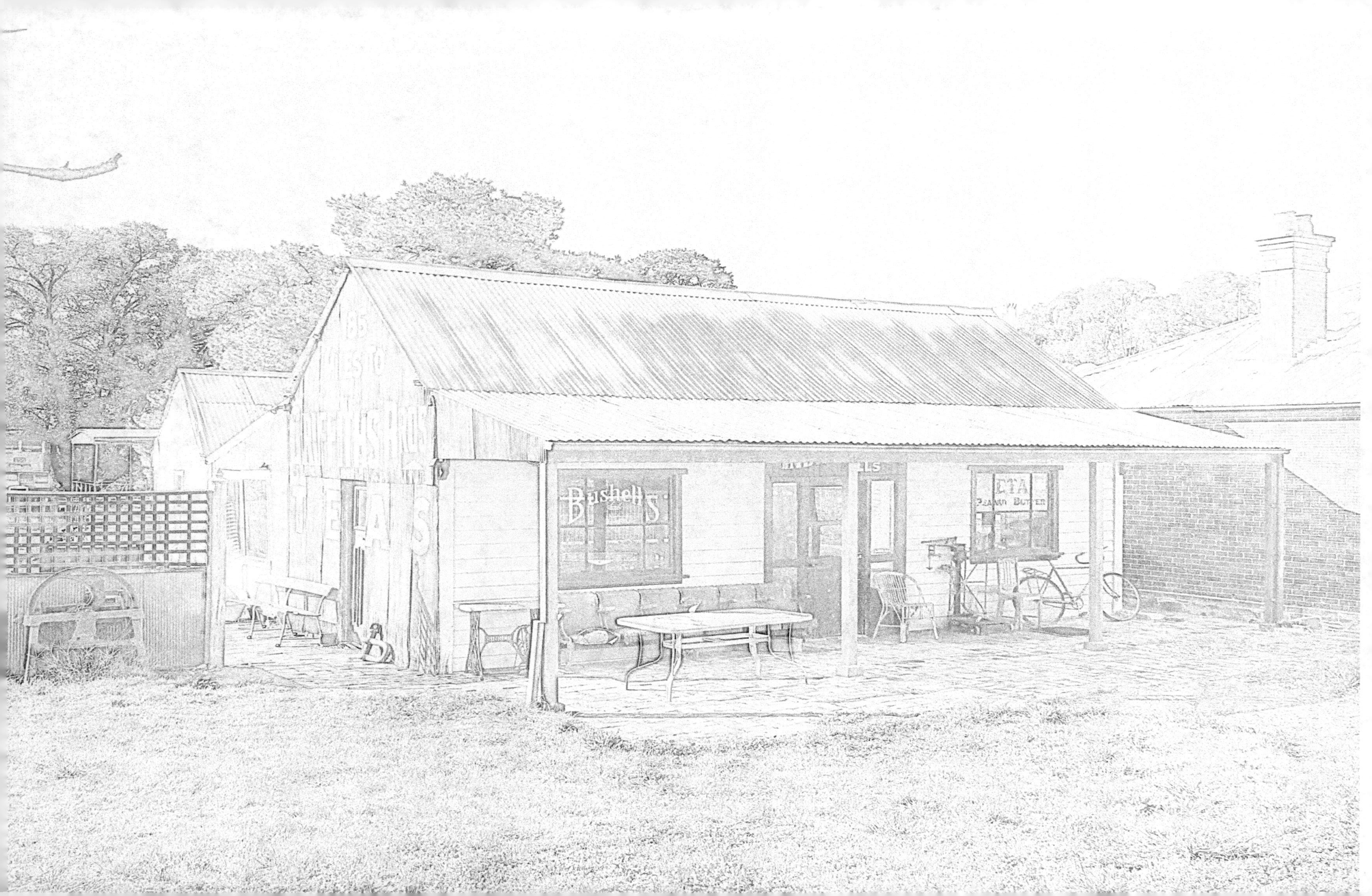
Bushell's
ETA
TEAS

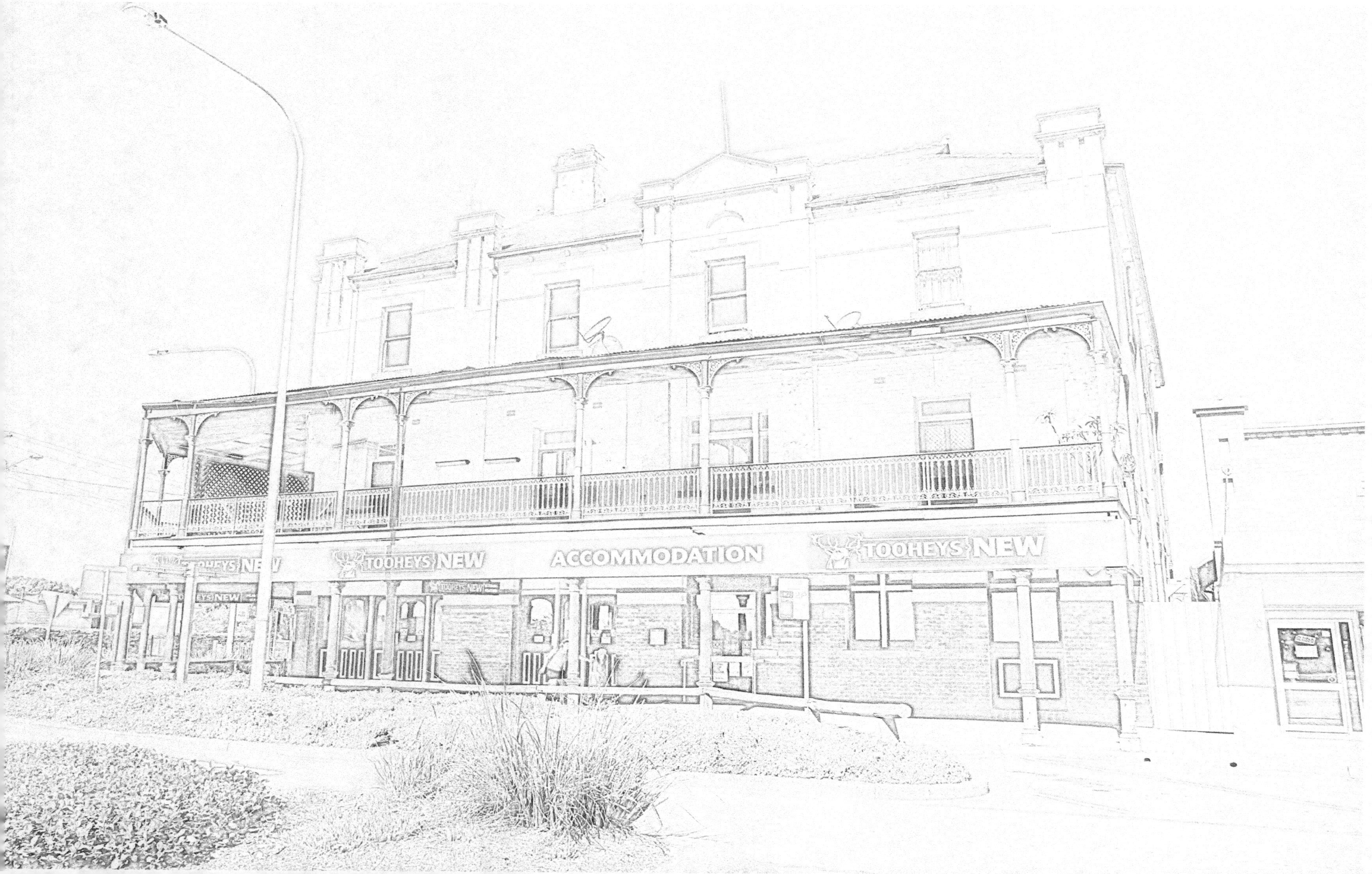
TOOHEYS NEW
ACCOMMODATION
TOOHEYS NEW
TOOHEYS NEW

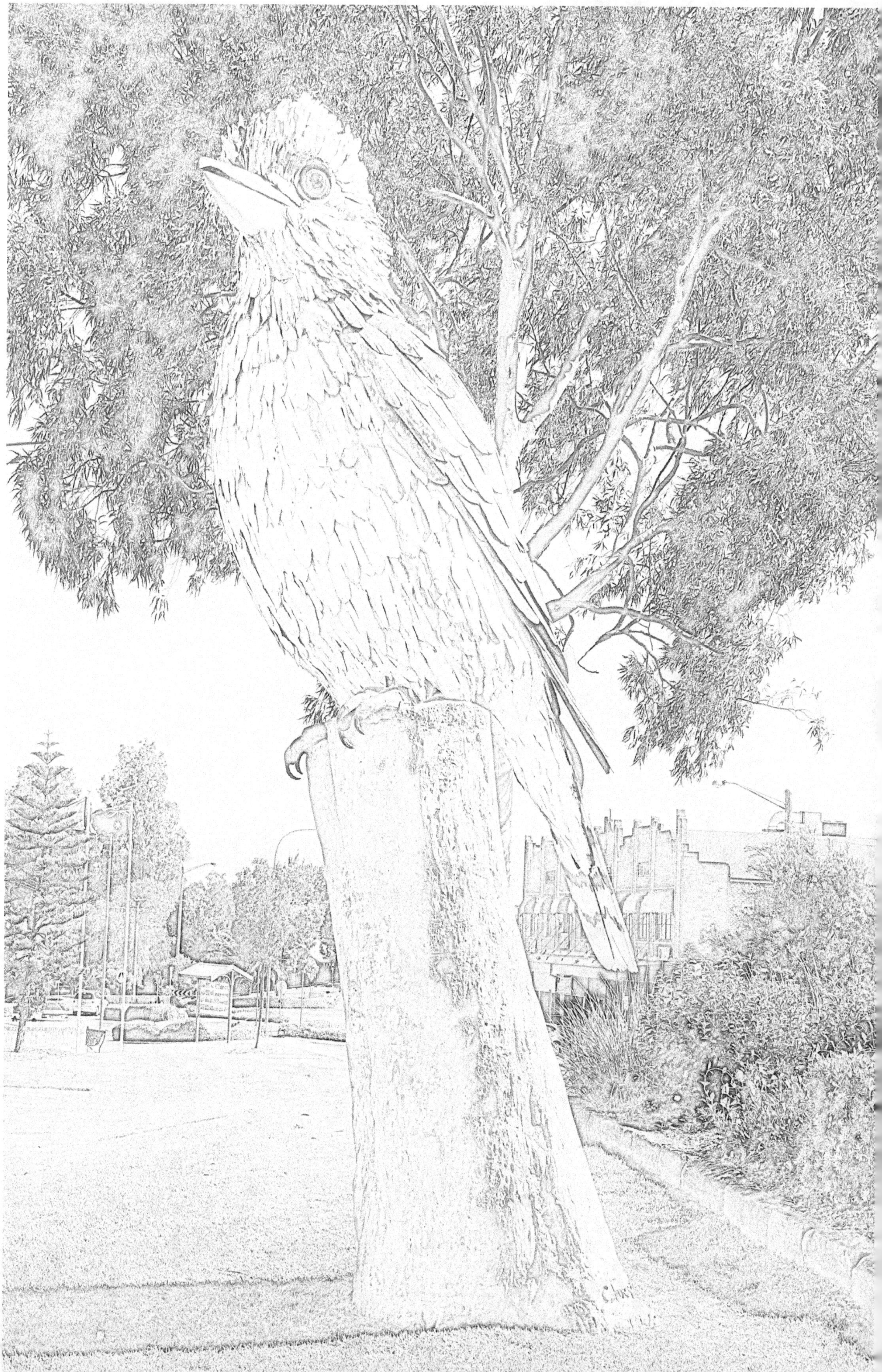

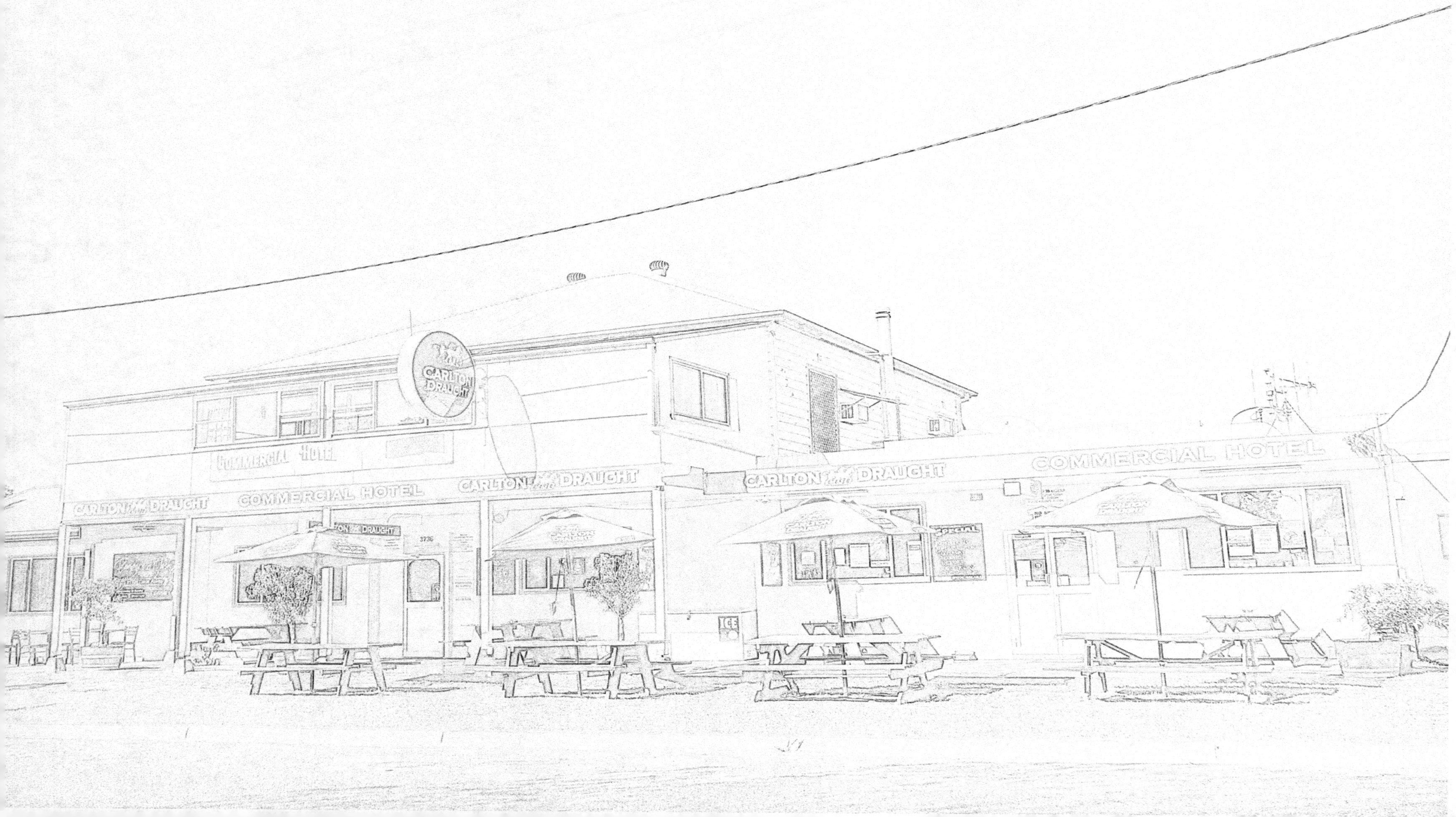
CARLTON DRAUGHT
COMMERCIAL HOTEL
CARLTON DRAUGHT
COMMERCIAL HOTEL
CARLTON DRAUGHT
CARLTON DRAUGHT
COMMERCIAL HOTEL
CARLTON DRAUGHT
3736
ICE

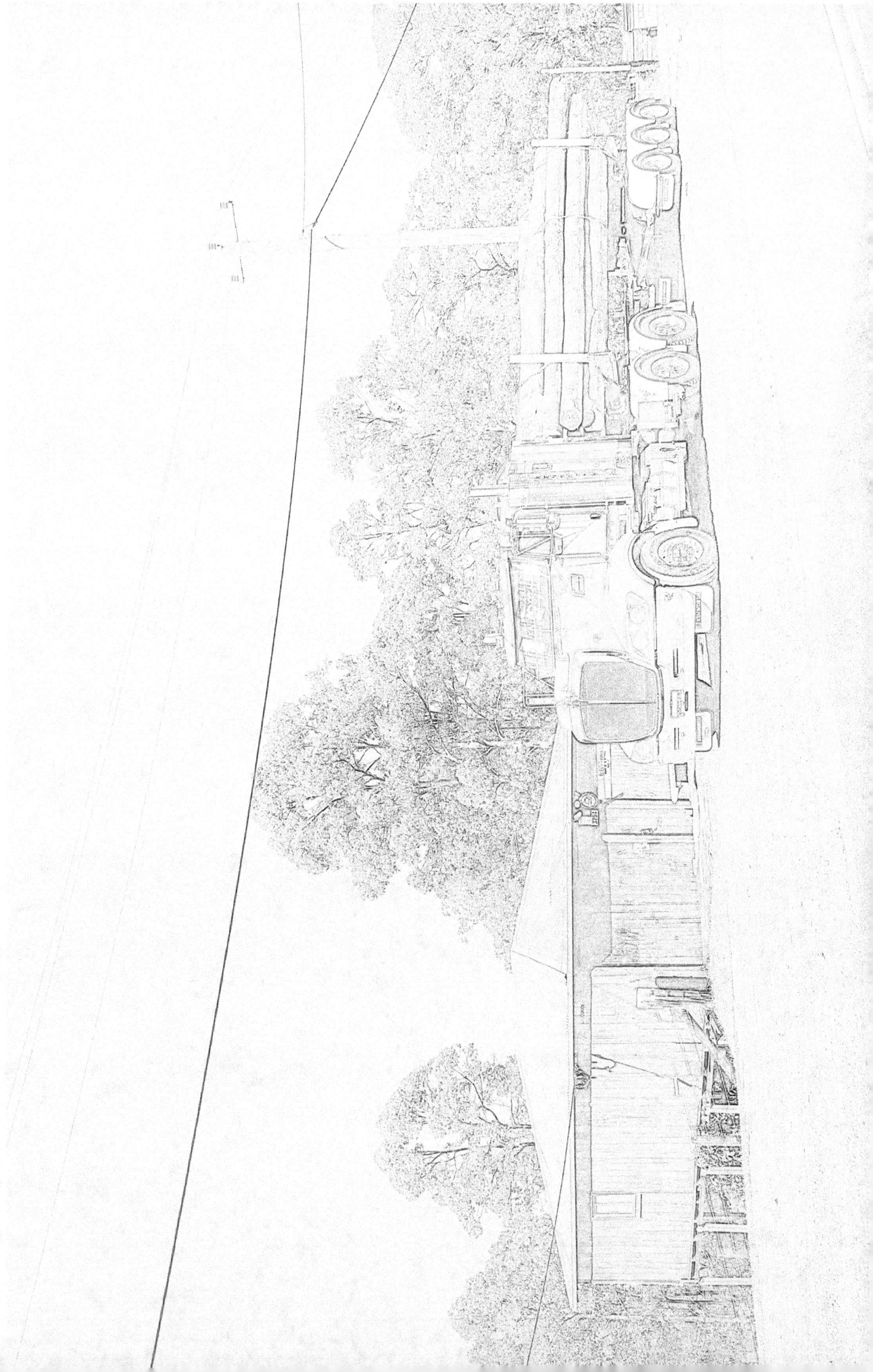

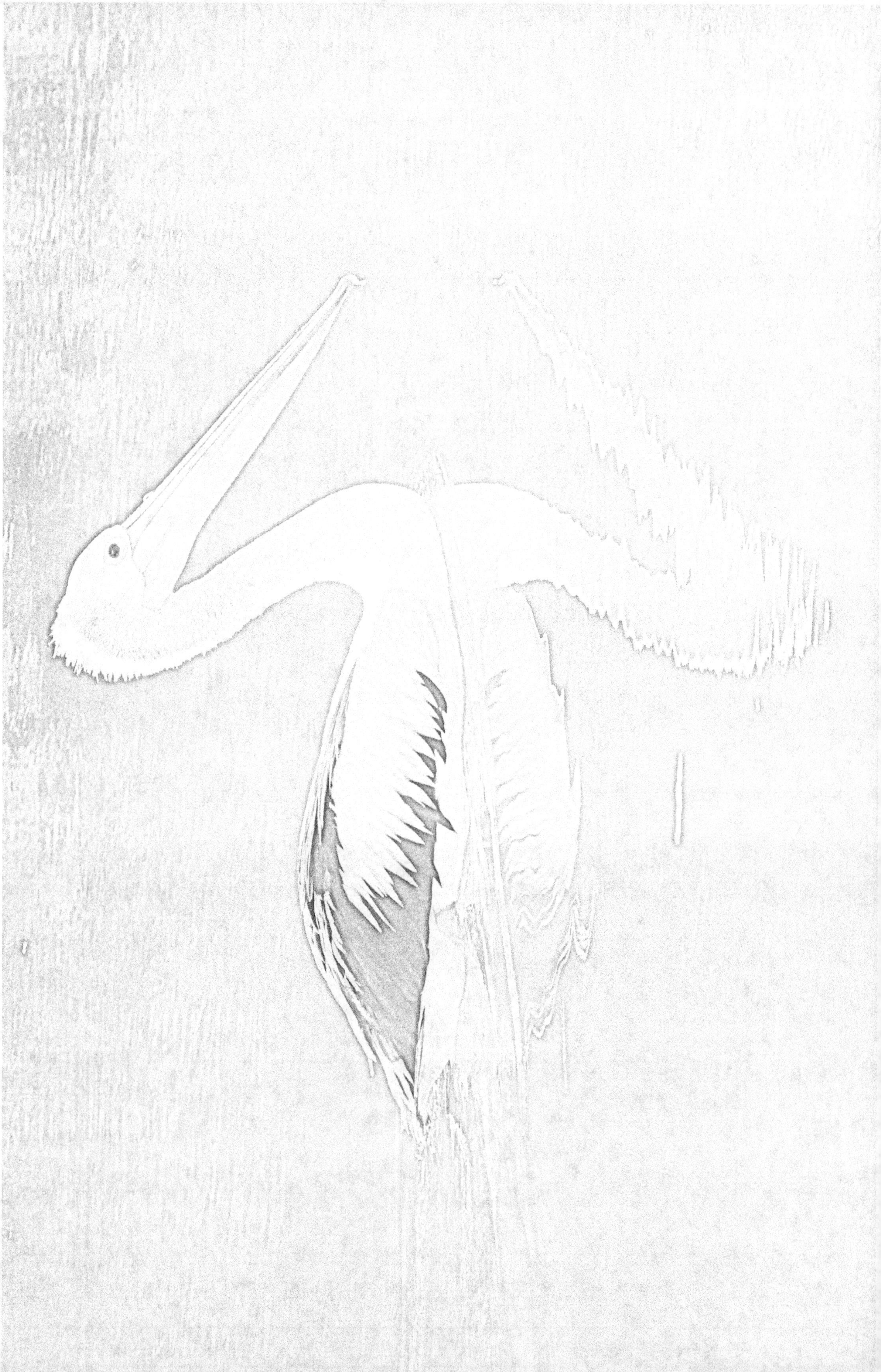

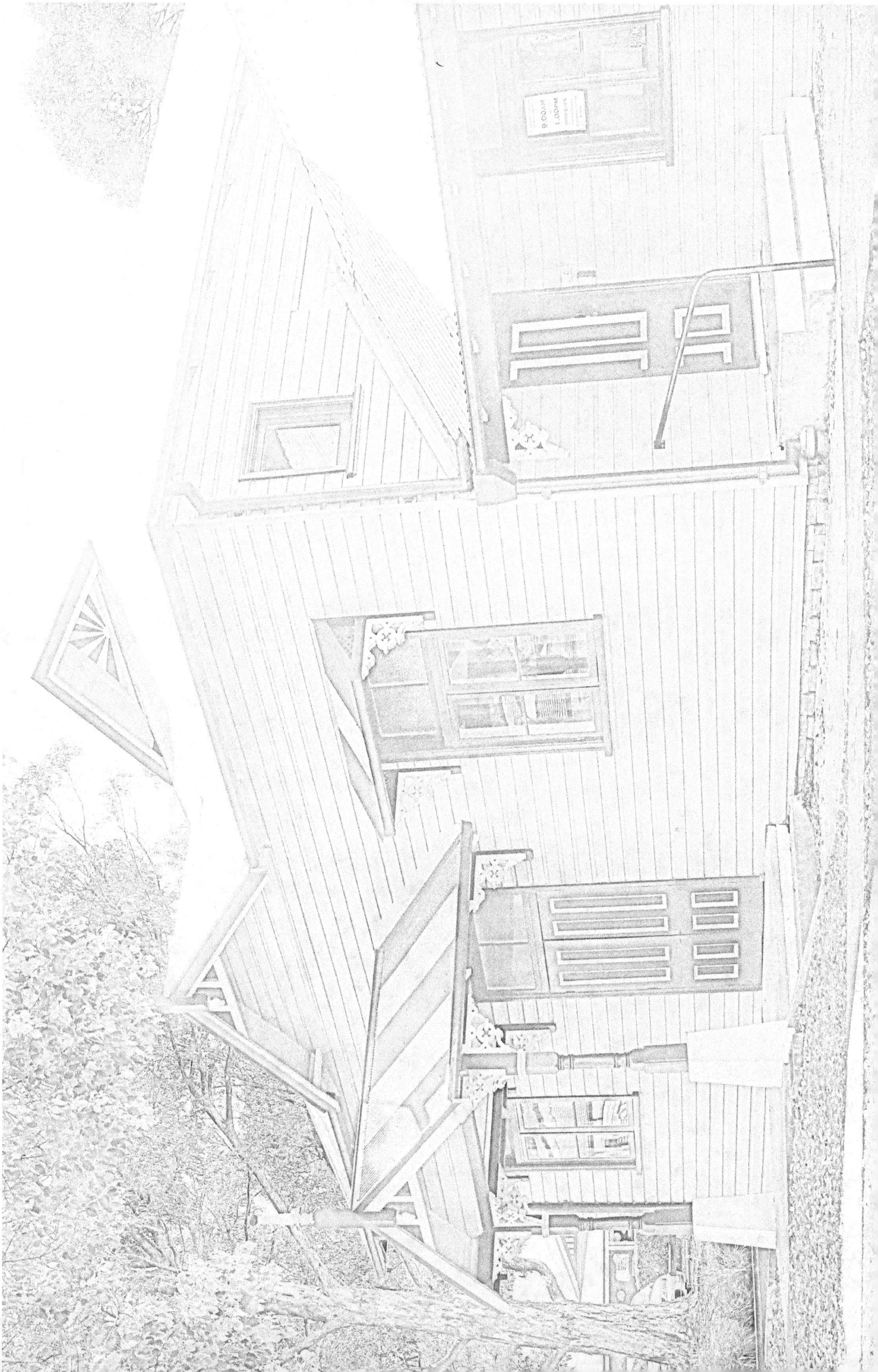

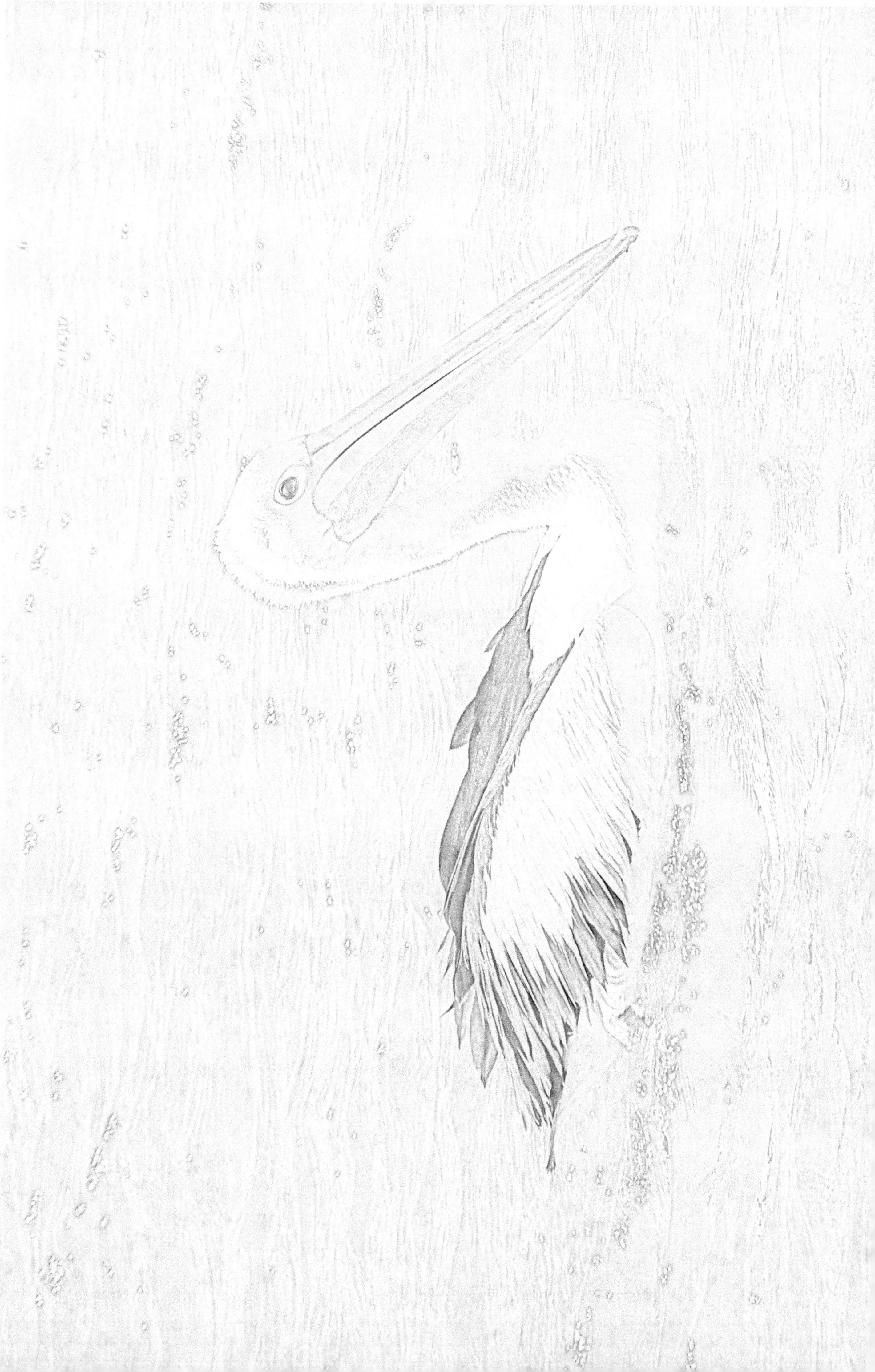

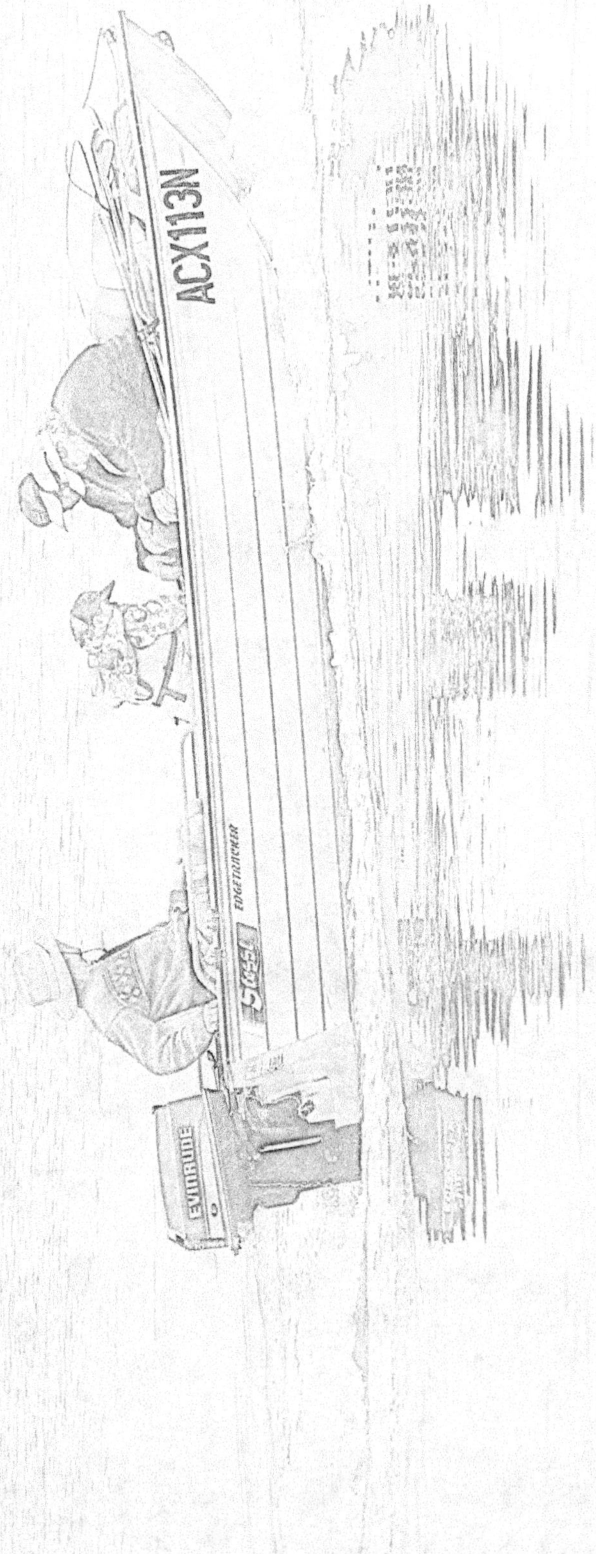
ACX113N
EVINRUDE

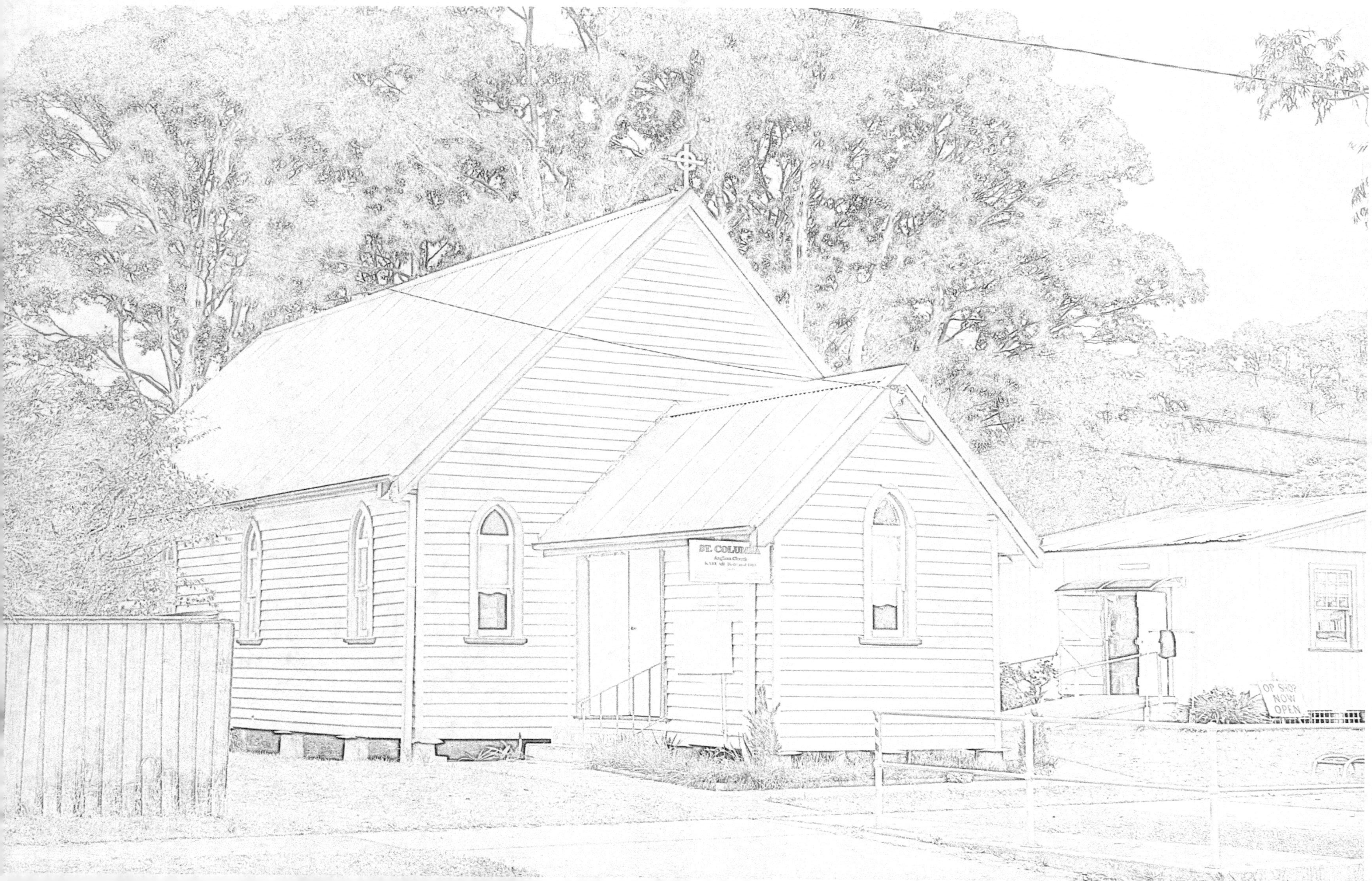
OP SHOP
NOW
OPEN

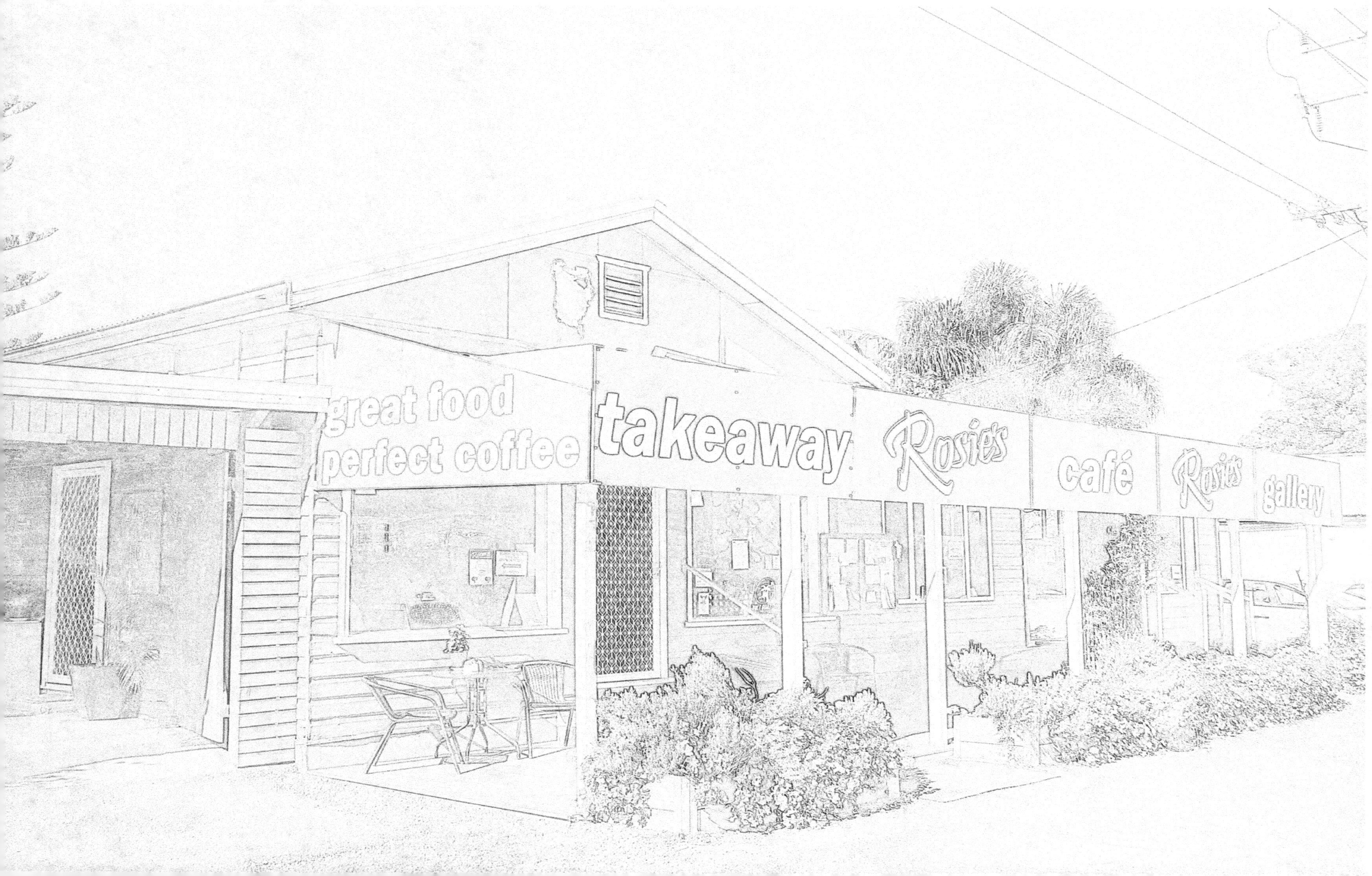
great food
perfect coffee
takeaway
Rosie's
café
Rosie's
gallery

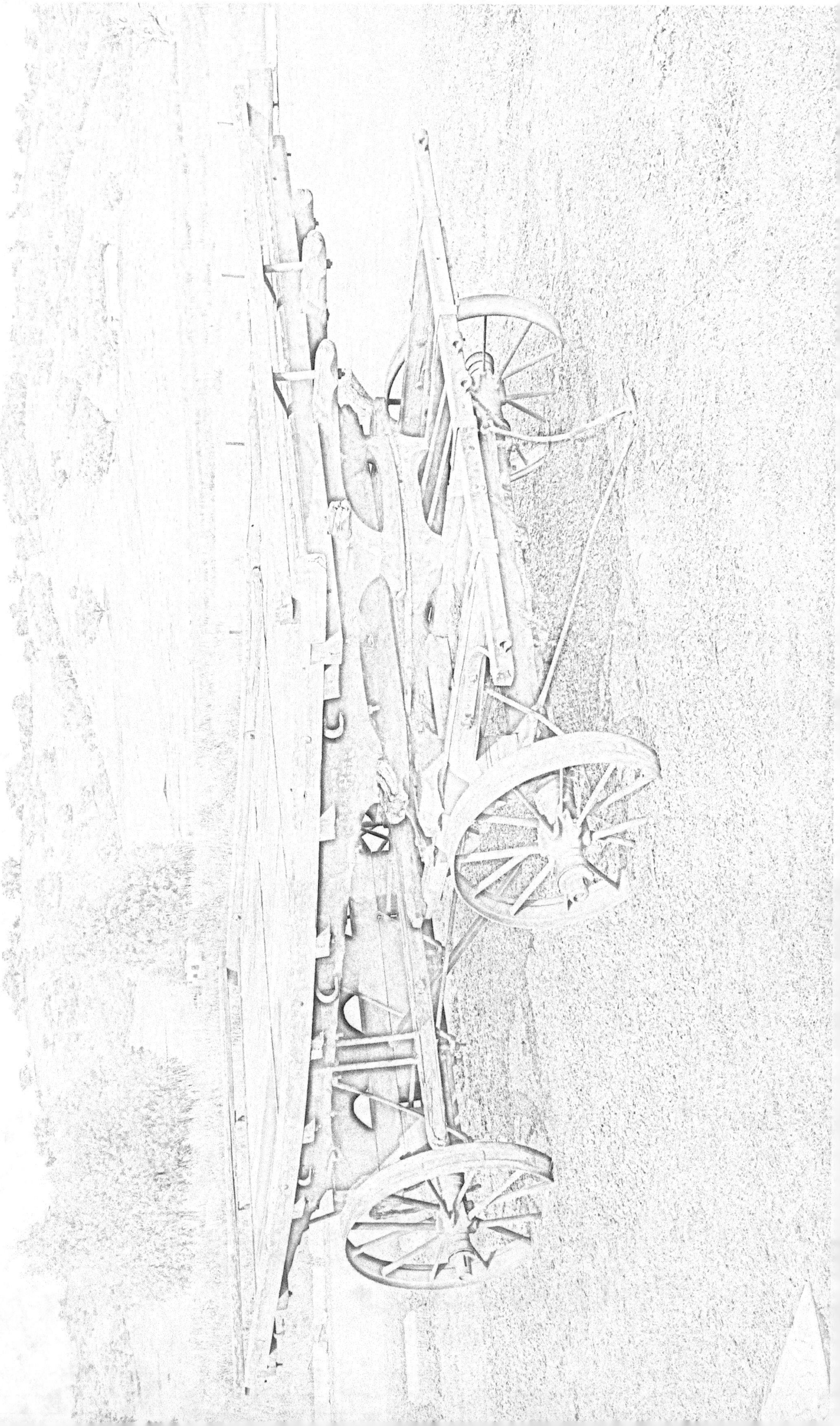

www.ingramcontent.com/pod-product-compliance
Lightning Source LLC
Chambersburg PA
CBHW081049180526
45170CB00005B/1742
* 9 7 8 0 3 5 9 8 0 1 5 6 5 *